TOO FRISKY!

**Also by Jim Davidson
and published by Robson Books**

TOO RISKY!

TOO FRISKY!

**Wicked Laughs
with the Ladies**

Jim Davidson

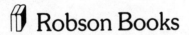 Robson Books

First published in Great Britain in 1988 by Robson Books Ltd,
Bolsover House, 5–6 Clipstone Street, London W1P 7EB

Illustrations © Chris Noton

British Library Cataloguing in Publication Data

Davidson, Jim, 1954–
  Too Frisky.
  1. Women – Humour
  I. Title
  305.4'0207

ISBN 0 86051 554 0

Printed in Great Britain by Billing & Sons, Worcester

Contents

INTRODUCTION

If you're working live on stage, trying to embarrass women in the audience is a sure way of getting them going. Men are dirty so and sos for the most part, but women try to remain prim and proper on the outside (though I'd love to be a fly on the wall of a ladies toilet). I know that deep down women laugh at the sort of things they'd never dream of laughing at in mixed company and I've had some really wicked laughs with women in my audiences if they haven't had their men with them.

I did a ladies night about ten years ago with five hundred women in the house. The things they were shouting out were disgusting. I haven't done a show like that since.

I find now that I like to go out on stage and get the feel for an audience rather than having any pre-set routine. I like to chat to them, coming up with whatever comes into my head. That way the act is always fresh and always different. No one knows from one night to the next what I'm going to say – least of all me.

Whenever I meet women I can't help but try to shock them in a way, to get a reaction. I've got a mate who's like that. He's absolutely disgusting with women, far worse than when he's with a group of men, but the girls love him for it.

Perhaps deep down inside, beneath all the streaked hair and jingly jangly bracelets, a girl likes a man to be a man, burps and all.

I think women drivers are slightly strange. Take my girl friend. We can be driving along and I can tell her to turn left . . . LEFT . . . and she'll turn right. We drove into town once to look round the shops and she got so frustrated and flustered when she couldn't park the car in a space that she turned and drove straight back home. She wouldn't park it because I'd got on her nerves telling her how to drive.

Shocking women is one thing, but I don't go out of my way deliberately to upset them in the audience. Occasionally there's the odd one who takes real offence at something I say, but for every one like her there are hundreds of others who like the chance just to let their hair down and have a really good laugh along with everyone else – usually over subjects they'd never dare mention openly.

That's why I hope you'll enjoy the selection that follows.

FRISKY
FILLIES
AND
CUDDLY
KITTENS

I reckon to most blokes little girls seem to grow up almost overnight – the dividing line between childish innocence and stunning sex kitten is so thin. You've only got to look at some of the teenagers hitting the headlines at the moment to see that.

My act is always billed as an adult show (it has to be because of some of the stick it's come in for, but the audiences love it and you can't argue with the box office returns). Still, this means that I don't have to worry about kids being in the audience. If you know there are families out there with youngsters you're always more careful about what you say on stage. I've got a teenage daughter myself and know all about what it's like trying to bring them up. I suppose it's the rule as much as anything else, but you can't help being concerned about them.

Girlish innocence is always good for a laugh though. As I say sometimes in the show, 'Do you know the difference between a man's dick and a leg of chicken?'

'No,' says the girl.

'All right them, do you want to come on a picnic?'

So to start with, here's a collection of gags and jokes all about innocence and experience and what happens when the two come up against each other!

A baby boy and a baby girl were sleeping together in a cot when suddenly the girl started yelling, 'Rape! Rape!'

'Oh, be quiet,' said the little boy. 'You just turned over on to the end of my dummy.'

Did you hear about the teenage girl who found a frog in a ditch? She took it home, climbed into bed with it, kissed it and it turned into a handsome prince.

No ... her mother didn't believe it either.

Prim young Deborah was rather strapped for cash when one day she happened to be walking past some allotments on the edge of town and saw to her surprise a Ferrari parked near one of the plots. Curious at such an obvious sign of wealth in a poor part of town, she asked a passer-by who it belonged to.

'That belongs to old Bill,' said the man. 'He's got the plot next to mine. He's over there if you want to talk to him,' and he pointed to a shambling old figure in the distance.

So Deborah went over to Bill and complimented him on his wonderful car. 'But please tell me,' she said, 'how on earth can you afford it?'

'I do a bit of betting on the quiet,' said Bill, 'and that brings in a little cash now and then.'

'What sort of bets?' asked Deborah. 'They must be very large.'

'All sorts,' said Bill. 'For example – I bet you £100 that by next Saturday morning you'll have a big black boil on the top of your thigh.'

'That's silly,' she told him. 'You'd never win on a bet like that!'

'Want to try?' asked Bill, with a glint in his eye.

Deborah thought about it a moment, realized it was easy money and agreed. Each of them wrote out a cheque for a hundred pounds and left it with the neighbouring plot owner for safe keeping.

The week passed and Deborah made sure she kept an eye on her skin, avoiding any soaps or perfumes that might cause an allergy. As Saturday approached she thought more and more how much she wanted that hundred pounds – and how easy it was.

Saturday arrived, she checked her legs and went off to meet Bill as arranged. 'The money's mine,' she told Bill proudly. 'There's no boil at all.'

'I'd like to take your word for it,' said Bill, 'but with so much money at stake I ought to make sure. Would you mind just dropping your jeans and knickers so I can check.'

Deborah was taken aback at this, but reckoned old Bill was a harmless enough old boy, and she wasn't going to quibble for a hundred quid. So she quickly dropped her knickers to reveal an exquisite arse and fanny – but no sign of a boil.

'All right,' said Bill, 'the money's yours. Here's your hundred pounds.'

'You're crazy,' said Deborah as she zipped herself up. 'How can you make money if you lose on silly bets like this?'

'Easy,' replied Bill. 'You see those flats over there? Well, I bet my mates there £200 that I'd have your knickers off by noon today.'

One young girl said to another, 'Well, was he the perfect date?'

'Not quite,' replied her friend. 'He was tall, dark and all hands . . .'

A horny young girl had just returned from a day's sailing with her new man. 'Wasn't it just super out there on the water?' said Mark.

'Isn't it just super *anywhere?*' replied the girl.

Did you hear about the teenage girl who was so poor she said she'd do anything for a new coat? Now she can't do it up over her stomach . . .

Two schoolgirls were talking about the facts of life. 'Do you smoke after sex?' asked one of them.
'I've no idea — I've never looked,' said her pal.

Susie was a well-built young girl who was going to her first 'grown up' party. She chose to wear a low-cut dress with a necklace that had a pendant in the shape of a helicopter. Not long after she arrived at the party, Susie noticed an attractive young man who kept staring at her and especially at her necklace.

After this had been going on for some time, she walked across to him and said, 'I'm glad you like my little helicopter.'

'It's not that, darling,' he replied. 'I was just admiring its landing strip.'

A young inexperienced girl was being chatted up by a fast-talking journalist. 'I'll be straight with you,' said the hack. 'I've only got a few hours in town, so do you screw or don't you?'

'Well,' said the girl, blushing, 'not normally, but you've talked me into it.'

Did you hear about the young girl with only one thing on her mind? She thought Moby Dick was a sexual disease.

An innocent young girl from a family living on a housing estate was going out with a very posh young man when, alas, she became pregnant.

Her dad was beside himself and gave her boyfriend a right talking-to.

'It's quite all right,' said the wealthy beau. 'I'll make sure your daughter's OK. If she has a boy she'll get £50,000 and if it's a girl, she'll get £40,000.'

'And if she should miscarry,' said the father, changing his tune. 'Would you give her a second chance?'

A pretty young thing was being pestered by a man squeezed up behind her as they travelled in a busy tube train. 'Look,' she hissed, 'will you just stop poking that thing into my backside.'

'I'm very sorry,' said the man with a grin, 'but it's only my pay packet.'

'Then you're obviously very good at your job,' hissed the girl again as she felt another prod in her back, 'because that's your fourth rise in the last twenty minutes!'

Two prim but pretty young girls were talking. 'You'll never guess what happened to me on the train,' said Sue. 'I was sitting alone in a compartment when this tall, dark, handsome man came in.

'Well, he was very charming and we soon got talking. He sat next to me and soon he was blowing into my ear and kissing my neck.'

'What happened next?' asked Jane.

'After a while he slipped his hand inside my jumper, undid my blouse and started caressing my breasts.'

'And then?'

'Well, then he took off my bra and panties and started stroking between my legs while he held his "thing" in one hand and asked me to kiss it.'

'And what then?' asked Jane breathlessly.

'Hey, what kind of girl do you think I am?' replied Sue angrily. 'I pulled the alarm cord, of course.'

An attractive young girl was walking alongside a swimming pool clad in only the briefest of bikinis.

'Wow!' said a young hunk. 'Come over here so I can look a little longer.'

'No way,' said the girl with a brief smile as she fled, 'from where I'm standing you're looking a little longer already.'

Nina had just come home from her first date. Ecstatic, she tossed off her clothes and threw them round the room before diving into bed. In the morning her big sister came into the room and asked the still snoozing girl, 'How did your date go?'

'Oh, it was wonderful,' said Nina dreamily.

'I guessed as much,' said her sister. 'Your knicks are still stuck to the ceiling.'

The vicar's son, Ben, was on the look out for a 'nice' girl but ended up at a really swinging party. However, after a while he spotted a pretty but plainly dressed young lady in a corner, who was obviously bored by what was going on round her.

Ben went over. 'Look,' he said, 'neither of us fits in here – can I take you home?'

'Of course,' said the girl. 'Where do you live?'

'My girlfriend is so ignorant about football,' Keith told his mate Charlie on their way to a match, 'she still thinks Sheffield Wednesday is a religious holiday.'

A young couple had just finished making love. 'I'm sorry, darling,' he murmured, 'if I'd known you were a virgin, I'd have taken a bit more time.'

'If I'd known we had more time,' snapped the girl, 'I'd have taken my knickers off.'

A young woman was eating at an outside table at a café when her mum came up and noticed her daughter wasn't wearing any underclothes.

'Why aren't you wearing any knickers?' she demanded.

'It helps keep the flies away from my food,' replied her daughter.

Young Suzie rushed into her elder brother's bedroom in a distraught state and told him, 'It's awful. I'm growing a brush between my legs.'

'What on earth are you talking about?' asked her brother.

'Look,' said Suzie, dropping her panties to show her first growth of pubic hair. 'See – I've got bristles.'

'Don't be stupid,' said her brother. 'Everyone has those – look,' and with that he dropped his trousers and pants.

'Oh, my God, that's even worse,' said Suzie. 'You've got the handle as well.'

Two teenagers, Lisa and Sharon, were having a chat. 'I feel worn out,' complained Sharon. 'I didn't get a wink of sleep until after four.'

'No wonder you're knackered,' replied Lisa. 'Just twice is enough for me!'

Two girls were sitting in a sleazy cinema watching a porn film when one said to her friend, 'Jane! Jane! The man next to me is wanking!'

'Well, just let him be,' said Jane.

'I can't,' said the first girl, 'he's using my hand.'

Three public schoolgirls, Lucy, Amanda and Clare, went off on their first big adventure together after leaving school – a safari in darkest Africa. One steamy tropical night Lucy was lying asleep alone in her tent when a huge ape burst inside, raped her and carried her off. Twenty-four hours later her friends found Lucy in a battered state and she was airlifted to hospital.

Some weeks later, back in Europe, Lucy finally began talking about her ordeal as her two friends sat beside her. 'Look, you must open up and tell us, what's wrong, what's going through your mind?' Amanda told her.

'What can I say?' wailed Lucy. 'He doesn't write, he doesn't call ...'

Why is a virgin the same as a haemophiliac? One prick and it's all over.

Anne was a super city slicker who was tired of 'meaningful' relationships and desperate for a good lay. She moved to a small town and put an ad in the local paper spelling out, quite bluntly, what her demands were: well-endowed young men who screwed well.

One night there was a tremendous ringing of the doorbell. She opened it to find a man there with no arms and no legs.

'I've come about the ad, madam,' said the cripple.

Anne was horrified and told him, 'I'm very sorry, but my advert was quite clear – and, to put it frankly, you don't appear to be all there.'

'Well, how do you think I rang the doorbell?' replied the man.

Julia had just left finishing school and was out for her first real evening on the town with a man. Her consort, Nigel, was eager to please and asked Julia what she wanted to do.

'Get weighed,' replied the young deb.

Not wanting to seem impolite, Nigel said OK and took her to an amusement arcade with a 'speak-your-weight' machine. They both had a go on it and after they'd finished Nigel again asked Julia what she wanted to do.

'Get weighed,' she replied again.

Puzzled, Nigel took her to a local fair where they found another weighing machine on which Julia duly measured her weight.

This went on a couple more times, after which Nigel was getting fed up. So he made an excuse about having to be up early in the morning, dropped Julia at her parents' house and gave her a peck on the cheek before speeding off in relief.

'How was your evening, darling?' asked Julia's mum.

'Wousy,' she answered.

Tracy was on her first date with a boy and they were parked in his car in a lay-by.

'God, it's so dark out here,' said the boy, 'I can't see my hand in front of my face.'

'There's no need to worry,' said Tracy, 'I know exactly where it is.'

Two tarts were walking down a street and without noticing passed a hairdresser's from which was coming a strong smell of singed hair.

''Ere, Debbie,' one said to the other, 'slow down a bit. I think we're walking too fast.'

The wealthy father of an attractive young woman, his only child, was dying and her parents were anxious for her to marry the right man to inherit the family money. Three men were considered to be suitable but she couldn't decide between them. So one evening she invited all three to her home and asked them to sleep in the same bed while she listened in from upstairs to hear who sounded the most promising.

The first man told the others, 'I must be up in time for my company's meeting tomorrow and we're announcing record profits.'

Upstairs the girl heard this and thought, 'He must be loaded. I'll marry him.'

But the second man in the bed started talking, 'Well, I must be in London in the morning, my Dad's signing over another 5,000 acres to add to my estates.'

And the girl thought, 'He's even richer! That's the one for me.'

Then the third bloke in the bed called out irritably, 'Move over you two, you're both lying on my cock.'

Upstairs the girl licked her lips and thought, 'My future husband!'

A well-stacked young lady was eyeing up the local talent on a beach. Turning to her friend, she said, 'You know, I'm really looking for a serious relationship. Someone I can spend the rest of my holiday with.'

'I wouldn't say my girlfriend was flat-chested,' said Sid to his mates, 'but she once got a job modelling for a firm who make fencing posts.'

Young Diana came home nervously one day and broke the news to her parents that she and her boyfriend were getting married.

Rather worried, as he hadn't met him, her father asked, 'Well, what's this young man like, anyway?'

'Oh, he's very nice,' said Diana. 'And he says that a good home has always been important to him . . .'

'Well, that sounds OK,' said her father, reassured.

' . . . And he says he likes the look of ours very much,' continued Diana.

Did you hear about the bimbo who had to give up using toilet water? She kept falling into the pan while trying to splash it on.

First Girl: **'Why do they call Debbie "Snow White"?'**
Second Girl: **'Because she's keen on shorts and Seven Up.'**

Two young women were at a museum admiring the works of art. They stopped in front of a statue of a magnificently built ancient Greek god, totally naked apart from a large leaf covering a massive bulge.

One of the women was impatient to move on, but her friend remained transfixed to the spot with her eyes on the statue.

'Come on,' said her friend sarcastically, 'what are you waiting for – Christmas?'

'No,' sighed her friend, 'autumn.'

Two young sisters discovered a pickled penis lying in an old jam jar. 'What shall we do with it?' asked Linda.

'I don't know,' said Sandra, 'but let's take it home.'

Anyway, they were lying in bed that night when Linda said, 'You know, it's very long isn't it? I'd like to have that pickled penis up my pussy.'

No sooner had she spoken than the penis leapt out of the jar and whooshed up Linda's fanny and satisfied her.

'That's marvellous,' said Sandra, 'it works by command. Let me have a go.'

So Sandra called out, 'Pickled penis, up my pussy,' and immediately the massive tool whooshed up inside her.

Well, the two girls had great fun playing with this until their big sister Jane, sleeping next door, was woken up by the laughter and moans of satisfaction. She came storming into the room shouting, 'What the hell's going on in here? Some people are trying to sleep.'

Linda and Sandra fell silent until they finally showed Jane the jam jar.

'And what's that supposed to be?' snorted Jane.

'It's a pickled penis,' Linda told her.

'Pickled penis?' said Jane scornfully. 'Pickled penis? Up my arse.'

Whoosh!!

Rachel, a randy young city girl, was on a farm holiday. One day she found herself surveying a herd of cattle with Derek, a well-built young farmworker.

Suddenly they saw an old bull climb up behind one of the cows and give the animal a good shafting with its massive tool.

'Phew!' said Rachel, coyly eyeing her companion and the bulge in his trousers, 'I wouldn't mind having a go at that myself.'

'Sure,' replied Derek. 'As soon as the old boy's finished I'll bring him over to you.'

Little Mandy was walking home early from school crying her eyes out. Sammy came up to her and asked, 'Why are you crying, Mandy?'

'Teacher says I've got to go home early because I'm bleeding.'

'Where? I can't see anything.'

'Between my legs. Here take a look,' and she lifted up her skirt and pulled down her knickers.

'Blimey, it's no wonder you're bleeding,' exclaimed Sammy. 'They've cut your willy off.'

Young Carol developed a sophisticated 'mind over matter' approach to sex. She doesn't mind and who the man is doesn't matter.

A sexy young eighteen-year-old was talking to her doctor a few days before she was going to have an operation. 'Do you think the scars will show?' she asked anxiously.

'That depends,' said the doctor, 'on what you take off.'

A buxom young blonde was on the telephone to the doctor's surgery. 'What, another thorough examination for tomorrow!' she exclaimed. 'But Dr Jones took a good look at me yesterday.'

'Yes,' replied Dr Black. 'He told me about that.'

Little Barbara was off on her first trip abroad by air. As the plane took off and gained height her mother glanced over at her. The little girl seemed puzzled.

'What do you think of it?' asked her mum.

'Fine,' said Barbara, 'but when will we start getting smaller?'

Two stable-lads watched admiringly as Miss Patricia, the young lady of the house, rode away on her big black hunter.

It was late in the afternoon when she returned. The horse was sweating heavily and looked exhausted.

'He looks shagged out,' said one of the lads as they were rubbing down the panting beast.

'So would you,' said his mate, 'if you'd spent the whole day between those thighs.'

Over coffee, young Kate was boasting to Maureen that she had a date with a bloke who was well-known for the great size of his organ. Maureen congratulated her, but then went to the cupboard and brought back a tape measure and a felt tip.

'Why are you giving me all this?' asked Kate in surprise.

'Well, dear,' said Maureen, 'with a man like that you have to know where to draw the line.'

When she was propositioned by a wealthy Arab at a cocktail party, young Fiona thought of an easy excuse. 'I'm sorry,' she explained to Abdul, 'but I'm on my menstrual cycle.'

'That's no problem,' said Abdul. 'One of my men will ride it round to my place in the morning.'

Diana and Patricia were going away on holiday with their boyfriends for the first time. That night at the hotel they decided to compare notes on their boyfriends' prowess and agreed to chalk up a running 'score' on the outside of their bedroom doors, so they could keep a check on each other.

Later that night Diana had just chalked '4' on the outside of her door when she decided to go to Patricia's room to see how she was faring. To her amazement she saw '111' written in chalk on the door.

Banging on it loudly, she screamed through the keyhole, 'For God's sake slow down, or you'll set the hotel on fire!'

A little boy and a little girl were comparing their respective sex organs. 'Look at this,' said the little boy, fingering his willy. 'Daddy says the bigger it is the prouder a man should be.'

'That's not true,' replied the little girl. 'Mummy says that when it grows big all a man wants to do is hide it inside a woman's.'

Florence was on her first heavy date with a man and decided to keep in touch with her older, more experienced pal, Carol, by way of a little walkie-talkie. So while Carol stayed in an upstairs room, Florence was able to give her a blow by blow account of what was going on.

'Here goes,' she whispered late in the evening to Carol, 'he's undressing.'

'That's OK,' replied Carol. 'Just tell me how it progresses.'

At that point the man took off his shirt.

'He's got a hairy chest,' said Florence.

'Great,' said Carol. 'Carry on.'

A few minutes later Florence came on the air saying, 'He's got very strong thighs.'

'Sounds good. Carry on.'

Just then the man took off his pants and Florence saw a huge scar running from his crutch. 'Christ,' she whispered into the radio, 'it stretches right round his back.'

'Just hold on,' whispered Carol, 'I'm coming down – sounds like he's got enough for both of us!'

Did you hear about the two inexperienced cow-girls who failed to get Daisy in calf? They couldn't get her to lie on her back when the bull came.

The headmistress's daughter was a real tomboy and always getting into scrapes in and around the private school's grounds. One day she leapt off a tree on to a fence and cut her pussy quite badly.

She was rushed into the sickroom where the school doctor prepared to sew it back up for her. 'Before I do,' said the doc, 'what size would you like me to make it?'

'The same size as my mother's,' said the young girl.

'In that case,' said the doctor, packing away his instruments, 'just go out and jump off that tree three more times!'

Little Cindy had gone out to stay with her rich uncle and aunt in their country house. Coming from a poor inner-city area she found it all new to her, and she constantly asked questions about what this was, what that was called and so on. She particularly admired her uncle's collection of antelope and lion heads from his Big Game days in Africa. One day she saw something she didn't recognize on the hall table.

'What are they, uncle?' asked Cindy.

'They're a couple of golf balls.'

Well, the time came for Cindy to go home. But next year she returned to the country again for another holiday. As she came into the hall she noticed four golf balls lying on the table. 'Oh look, uncle,' she exclaimed delightedly, 'you've shot another golf!'

A mother was trying to comfort her young daughter who came home in floods of tears.

'What's the matter?' asked the mother.

'Mummy, it's Timmy.' And she pointed to her pussy. 'He's got something I haven't got.'

'There's no need to worry,' said her mum with a sigh. 'As long as you've got one of these you'll always be able to get one of those.'

Daphne was discussing her new boyfriend with her friend Louise. After a while the friend got a bit pissed off with Daphne constantly singing his praises. 'Yes,' she hissed, 'but tell me Daphne – what does he actually do for a living?'

Daphne was taken aback. 'Er, I'm not sure ... but I think he must be a doctor.'

'What do you mean, he must be a doctor?' said her friend.

'Well, he's so clever,' replied Daphne, 'he's already cured me of that horrid bleeding I used to get once a month.'

IN AND OUT OF THE NEST

The next time I get married I'm getting married first thing in the morning. Then if the marriage doesn't work, it doesn't mess the whole day up!

Most of the audiences in my summer shows are made up of couples on holiday, in Torquay or wherever I'm playing. And you can always get an audience like that going by rubbing up the men and their wives. I ask the blokes how many fellows think of someone else when they're making love to their wives. You can see them squirming in their seats and saying, 'Don't even mention it, Jim.'

All the girls start laughing and smack their husbands.

Then I ask them, 'How many of you girls still play with yourselves while your husband's at work?'

That sort of evens things up and gets them all laughing.

If I'm talking to a group of girls on their own in the audience I'll ask them where their husbands are. They always answer they're at home.

'No, they're not,' I tell them. 'They're down the pub pulling something. They're out doing it. Men are not faithful.'

The best thing a bloke can do if he's out for the evening is put a piece of white chalk in his top pocket, then if his wife starts on at him asking, 'Where have you been till this hour?' he can tell her, 'I've been out with a couple of birds having an orgy.'

'You lying bastard,' she says. 'You've been out with your mates playing darts.'

Marriage is a funny old game, when you think about it.

Finding out what someone's really like and living with them can be bloody hard at times. If you can put humour into a marriage, you're laughing (literally). You get these wives who want a nine to five bloke. Give it to them, I say. Go out at nine and come home at five o'clock in the morning!

Finding fun in marriage and in the embarrassing situations that married couples get themselves into is always popular with audiences and jokes like these get a packed house roaring their heads off.

Farmer Giles was smashed out of his head and lying next to his wife in bed. "Ere, Joan,' he said slowly, 'just think. If you could lay eggs we wouldn't have to feed no hens.'

'And just think,' replied his wife, 'if you could lay me, we wouldn't have to feed your brother Tom so often!'

Sam got halfway to work when he realized that he'd left an important document at home. As he went through the front door he noticed his wife, dressed only in a skimpy dressing-gown, bending over the kitchen table cleaning it. Aroused by the sight, he went up to her and without a word lifted the dressing-gown and 'pleasured' her furiously from behind.

'Well,' he panted as he finally came, 'haven't you got anything to say?'

'Oh ... thank you,' murmured his wife dreamily, ' ...and can you leave an extra pint?'

Doctor: 'What's the problem, Mr Smith?'
Patient: 'It's my wife's arms.'
Doctor: 'How do you mean, your wife's arms? What's wrong with them?'
Patient: 'I keep finding other men in them.'

It was the grudge village cricket match of the season and Billy was playing a storming innings, knocking the opposition bowlers all over the ground. At one point he saw a funeral procession passing the ground and immediately took off his cap and bowed his head as it passed. After a moment's hesitation, the other players followed suit.

At the end of the over, the visiting skipper told him, 'That was one of the most touching gestures I have seen on a cricket field.'

'It was the least I could do,' replied Billy. 'I'd been married to her for thirty years.'

Hear about the doctor's wife who had to go away for a week? She left seven apples on the au pair's bed.

A long-suffering wife was out in a boat with her errant husband one day when the small craft suddenly sprang a leak. Desperately the man searched the bottom of the boat looking for the source of the water, but he couldn't find it.

'That's typical,' said his wife as they started to sink. 'If the hole had hair on it, you'd find it fast enough.'

A husband came home early from work and found his wife in bed with their doctor. 'What in God's name do you think you're doing?' he stormed.

'I'm ... I'm taking your wife's temperature,' stammered the doctor.

'OK,' said the husband. 'But I hope for your sake that thing's got numbers on when you take it out!'

Two middle-aged women are sitting on the bus. One turns to the other and says, 'I can't help noticing what your eldest daughter is doing these days, Mrs Jones.'

'Really,' says Mrs Jones. 'What's that?'

'Well, Mrs Jones,' replies the first woman, 'she's taken up knitting – you know ... small clothes!'

'Well, thank heavens for that,' declares Mrs Jones with a sigh. 'Before that she was always running round with strange men.'

One fine morning a Scots grandmother decided to take her wee grandson, Jimmy, down to look at the sea. She dressed up the three-month-old boy and they went for a stroll along the front.

Suddenly a freak wave swept in and in a fraction of a second whisked little Jimmy out to sea.

The old lady was horrified and began loudly cursing the Almighty. 'Call yourself God?' she cried. 'That boy's mother has nursed him in the womb and he's only just three months old. What chance has he had to learn about life? What an awful tragedy to inflict on a family.'

At that, a second large wave swept over the front and little Jimmy was returned, unharmed, to his grandmother's feet.

Without stopping to pick him up, she stared into the sky again and yelled, 'And he was wearing a hat as well!'

An old country gent was convinced that his young wife was having an affair but couldn't find any evidence. One morning, to console himself, he went out early to play a round of golf on the course near his home. On the second hole he met another man playing on his own and they decided to team up for the rest of the course. On the fourth hole the old buffer noticed to his surprise that his companion was carrying a rifle with his golf clubs and asked what it was doing there.

'Oh, I'm an assassin by profession,' said the other man casually. 'I always keep a gun handy.'

'Really? And those sights on top, I suppose they help you aim better?'

'Of course,' said the assassin, 'they're really powerful. Here, take a look.'

So the country gent peered through the sights and looked around until he almost dropped the gun in horror. 'Good God – I can see my wife in the bedroom and she's standing there with our neighbour,' he said outraged. 'The swine, they must be having an affair. Look, you're a paid killer,' he said turning to the assassin, 'will you do a job for me?'

A rich housewife was briefing the new au pair on how to prepare dinner for her husband that night. 'Now, tell me,' said the woman, 'are you sure you can cope if my husband should demand anything unexpected after the main course?'

'No problem,' said the au pair. 'I'm on the pill.'

But the assassin said that it was his day off, that he was enjoying a game of golf and didn't really want to work.

'I'll pay you a thousand pounds,' said the old man. 'In fact, one thousand for her and a thousand for him.'

The assassin was persuaded and agreed to do the job for a thousand each and carefully loaded a couple of bullets into the rifle. Before he took aim he said to the old boy, 'Look, you're paying me a thousand a bullet, so I'll give you a bit extra. Just tell me where you want me to hit them.'

'Well,' said the old boy, 'she's nagged me for the last five years, so hit her in the mouth. And him? He's having it off with my wife, so get him in the balls.'

Taking careful aim, the assassin peered through the sights and then suddenly said to the old boy, 'Hey, you're in luck. I think I can save you a thousand quid.'

A few days before his wedding a young man was enjoying his stag night and he and his mates picked up a couple of tarts. They had a great time, but one of the women gave him such a vigorous blow job in the back of her car that she injured his penis and he had to go to hospital. The doctor treated it, but said the man would have to wear a bandage on it for a week. Anyhow, the wedding went ahead, they had the reception and he found himself in the honeymoon suite with his bride for their first night together. As she cuddled up to him, she whispered, 'Darling, you know that I am innocent and have saved myself all for you – and I hope you are too.'

Blushing, the bridegroom said, 'Of course I am, darling.' And with that he dropped his trousers and pants saying, 'Look – it's so untouched it's still got the wrapper on.'

A pair of honeymooners were lying dreamily in each other's arms one morning. 'Last night I had a very strange dream,' Sophie said to Peter. 'I was at a prick auction and all the lots were divided into small, medium, large or extra large.'

'Really?' asked Peter nervously. 'Er ... did you see mine there?'

'Oh no,' said Sophie loyally. 'Your prick was too large to get in the auction room.'

Smiling at this, Peter admitted, 'Actually, I dreamed last night that I was at a fanny auction. They were divided into tight, medium, large and extra large.'

'Gosh, did you see mine there?' asked Sophie.

'See it? See it?' exclaimed Peter. 'The bloody auction was held in it.'

You know, incompatibility isn't such a problem in a marriage – as long as he has the income and *she* has the patability.

Mother to a virginal bride, 'Listen, take my advice. If you want your wedding night to be one to remember, give your new husband ten oysters to eat before you settle down.'

The day after the wedding the bride was in tears. 'What's the matter?' asked her mother. 'Didn't you give him the oysters?'

'Yes,' said her daughter, 'but only four of them worked.'

Mrs Booth-Taylor was desperate to keep up with her husband in everything he did and so started taking golf lessons because he was mad keen on the game.

She used to go out dedicatedly with the club pro to practise tee-shots, iron shots, putts – the full works, but all to no avail. Mrs Booth-Taylor was hopeless and could scarcely hit the ball.

In desperation the pro told her, 'Look, grip the club as if it was your husband's tool and then hit the ball.' To his amazement his pupil hit the ball 300 yards for a perfect shot.

'Brilliant!' yelled the prof. 'Now take the damned club out of your mouth and try again with your hands.'

A man was on the phone to a woman. 'Fancy a drink tonight?'

'I can't,' she replied, 'I've got to wash my hair.'

'Then how about tomorrow?'

'That's not any good either – I'm seeing my sister.'

'Well, what about lunch?'

'No, I've got to work right through today.'

'Surely this weekend must be free,' said the man, becoming increasingly exasperated.

'Er, no . . . I'm going to see my mother.'

'But your mother's dead.'

'It's my aunt, but she treats me as if I were her own.'

Really annoyed now, the man said, 'Look, I think you're just making excuses.'

'You said it.'

'Frankly, I sometimes wonder why we ever got married!'

A randy young wife was complaining to the other women in her church group that her man's tool was too small and said that she wanted to leave him. The others said that this was a serious matter and eventually it was agreed to put him to the test. The unfortunate husband had to dangle his manhood through a hole in the screen while the rest of the women considered its size.

Terrified at the prospect, and knowing that he wouldn't cut an impressive figure, he begged the vicar to take his place.

So, as the women gathered, the vicar thrust his massive member through the screen. Gasps of astonishment and delight greeted its appearance until one of the women standing at the back protested, 'But that's the vicar's dick. I'd know the birthmark on the side like the back of my hand.'

A notoriously randy salesman was sent round the country by his company, buying and selling. Each day he sent a telemessage to his long-suffering wife, 'Still moving. Still buying.'

This went on for a couple of long weeks until one day his wife sent a telemessage to the hotel where he was staying, 'Come back *now* – or I'll be selling what I'm damned sure you're buying.'

A woman was grumbling to a plumber about how long it was taking him to fix a dripping tap in her house. As she was giving him an earful he caught sight of her young son coming home, and hoping to change the subject said 'I remember your son – he was in the junior school when I did a job there.'

'Oh, yes,' snapped the mother, 'and what year was he in by the time you'd finished.'

A recently married young woman, who had a high-powered job as an executive in a big firm in the City, was being shown round a farm by an old farmer.

In one field they stopped to watch a bull coupling with not one but four different cows in the afternoon. 'That's what we call a working bull,' explained the farmer.

A little later the young woman watched enviously as this time they saw a stallion dishing out similar treatment to a group of obviously appreciative mares. 'That's what we call a working horse,' said the farmer.

Just then a lusty young woman came round the corner with a smile from ear to ear.

'Don't tell me,' said the City woman, 'she's married to one of your workmen!'

Old Joe was comforting his wife on her deathbed. All of a sudden Joan started weeping uncontrollably. 'Joe,' she sobbed, 'I have a confession to make. I slept with the milkman. I slept with your boss. And I slept with your best friend.'

'That's all right, darling,' said Joe softly. 'Why do you think I poisoned you?'

Jimmy was walking with his father one evening when they saw a couple of dogs hard at it on the pavement.

'What are they doing, Dad?' enquired the little lad.

'They're making puppies,' explained his father.

Later that evening, back at home, Jimmy rushed into his

parents' bedroom and caught them both naked, with his father bonking his spread-eagled mother.

'What are you doing, Dad?' exclaimed Jimmy.

Embarrassed, his father replied, 'Your mother and I are making babies.'

'In that case,' said Jimmy, 'turn her round and take her from behind. I'd rather have puppies.'

Two men playing a round of golf were held up at the fifth by a couple of women players ahead of them who were taking their time.

Eventually one of the men got so frustrated, he volunteered to go over and have a word with the two ladies. But he was back within seconds, red-faced and obviously disturbed. 'Good God,' he said to his partner, 'one's my wife and the other's my mistress. I can't possibly speak to them, you'll have to go.'

So the second man went over to speak to the two women, but he was also back within seconds and looking very red in the face. 'Well, what do you know . . .' he said to the other golfer.

After thirty years of non-stop work the boss of a Chinese takeaway decided he and his wife would take the night off, close the takeaway and spend the evening together.

So Mr Tong got in a bottle of wine and sat down with his wife on the sofa. For the first time in thirty years they were kissing passionately. A few minutes later, and again for the first time in a long time, Mr Tong slipped his hand inside his wife's blouse and fondled her breast. She sighed with contentment and responded by caressing his dick. This continued for a few minutes until Mr Tong leant over and whispered in his wife's ear, 'How would you like a 69?'

'Oh, darling,' she replied, 'why do you always have to talk about work?'

A hard-working but poorly-paid businessman came home early one day to find his wife in bed with another man, who was lying naked sprawled across the sheets.

The husband was about to explode with anger when his pretty young wife interrupted, 'Sweetheart ... remember that lovely new coat I got last year?'

'Yes,' he answered.

'Well, it was my lover who bought it, because we couldn't afford it. And he was the one who got me the new car and helped pay for the garage when we were gong through a bad time.'

'Christ,' said the husband in alarm. 'What do you think you're playing at? Get another blanket – he might catch a cold!'

A young man went to his doctor who realized at once that he was in a very disturbed state. 'Doctor, oh doctor, I've just got married,' said the patient, 'and I'm very worried about my new wife – she eats like a horse.'

'There's nothing unusual about that,' the doctor reassured him. 'Lots of young women have very hearty appetites.'

'But you don't understand. All she eats is rolled barley, oats, hay and buckets of water. She's got no interest in sex or anything else.'

'I see,' said the doctor, thinking it over. 'In that case she'd better have this,' and he filled out a form on his desk.

'That's great,' sighed the young husband with relief. 'Is that the prescription for her cure?'

'No,' said the doctor, 'it's a licence allowing her to crap in the streets.'

A young and very innocent rector had just married a horny spinster. As he prepared to get into bed on their wedding night, he knelt down and prayed, 'O Lord, please give me strength and direction.'

'Just you worry about your strength,' said his new bride. 'I'll take care of all the directing.'

Little Jimmy surprised his mum in the bath one morning. He pointed to her crutch and asked, 'What's that, Mummy?'

Struggling for a clever reply, mummy said, 'That's where your father hit me with a meat cleaver.'

'No kidding?' said Jimmy. 'Right in the pussy!'

A man was forced to work away from home for a few weeks. After a fortnight he couldn't contain himself any longer and visited a local brothel.

'Give me the worst lay you've got – here's ninety quid,' he told the madame.

The madame was stunned. 'You can get a very good lady for that money, you know,' she told him.

'Look,' replied the man, 'I'm not out for a good lay – I'm missing my wife.'

'Frank,' said a woman to her husband as he sped along in his brand-new car, 'I think you'd better slow down a bit. There's a motorcyclist with a flashing blue light behind us – and I think he wants to get past.'

A worried husband rushed home to his wife to tell her, 'Mavis, I've just heard that our neighbour has had every woman in the street except one.'

'That's right,' sneered Mavis. 'It's that snooty cow at number eleven.'

John: 'My wife drives like lightning.'
Fred: 'You mean she goes fast?'
John: 'No – I mean she's always splitting trees in half.'

Mark was proudly preparing for his big wedding day when to his dismay his best pal warned him not to marry Gloria. 'You just can't go through with it,' said his friend. 'She's been laid by every man in Southend.'

'Well,' said Mark defensively, 'Southend's not *that* big a town.'

Elizabeth and James were forced to spend their wedding night at her parents' house. As the young couple were undressing, innocent young Elizabeth noticed the hair covering James's back and chest. Distraught, she rushed out and went to her mum downstairs. 'It's awful,' she wept, 'he's got hair all over his body just like a chimp.'

'That's perfectly normal,' said her mother. 'Now get back upstairs and do your duty.'

This time Elizabeth watched as James took off his trousers and saw the hair on his legs. Once more she fled and complained to her mother, 'His legs are hairy too – just like an ape.'

Again her mother sent her back upstairs.

By now James had removed all his clothing and Elizabeth saw that part of his foot was missing and ran out hysterically for a third time to tell her mum, 'He's only got a foot and a half.'

Her mother replied, 'And you're complaining?'

Two suitors were vying for the hand of a beautiful young princess. One was old, fat and short-sighted. The other was tall, good-looking, young and very well hung.

It was decided that the two should compete for the princess by means of an obstacle race ending with a swim across a small lake.

The day of the contest loomed and the princess was confident that her young suitor would easily beat his fatter, slower rival. But shortly after they set off, disaster struck and the younger man fell over, hurting his leg. By the time the two rivals got to the lake they were still neck and neck. As they began swimming the younger man slowly began to overtake his rival, much to the princess's joy. But she decided not to take any chances and with the two men swimming towards her she took off all her clothes and posed provocatively to excite her favoured suitor to swim even faster. But to her horror he began swimming slower and slower, allowing the older man to overtake him and win by a few yards.

Later, as the ageing, fat suitor was celebrating his triumph, the furious princess turned on the younger man asking, 'What the hell happened to you? You were winning the race easily!'

'And so I was,' he replied, 'until you took off your clothes – and then I started dragging weed.'

A husband was very concerned about his wife's mental and physical condition and went to see their doctor. The doctor listened to the wife's symptoms and said to the husband, 'It's quite simple – your wife needs more physical contact. More sex. I'm prescribing more sex for her five times a week.'

'Great,' said the husband, 'I'll do Tuesdays and Fridays.'

Mrs Jones was aware that her husband had been feeling below par and arranged a check-up for him at the surgery. The doctor took some tests and as the husband had gone off to work, rang Mrs Jones at home with the results. 'I'm afraid it's very bad news,' he had to tell her. 'Your husband will be dead by the morning. Shall I break the news to him?'

'No, no,' she replied, stunned. 'I'll break it to him gently.' But instead she resolved to make his last hours as happy and carefree as possible. So when he got home in the evening Mr Jones found a drink ready and waiting, his favourite meal in the oven and his wife dressed sexily in a new dress. She made a big fuss over him and, after they had wined and dined, led him to the bedroom. There Mr Jones made passionate love to his wife not once but ten times. Still feeling randy, he turned to his exhausted wife and whispered, 'How about it just one more time?'

'It's all right for you,' she snapped irritably. 'You don't have to get up in the morning.'

One night disaster struck and the whole town was flooded. Everyone had to leave their houses and spend the night huddled in the town hall for shelter. At midnight a senior policeman walked in and asked, 'Are there any pregnant women here?'

'Do us a favour,' replied one drenched woman, 'we've only just got here.'

There was a primary school teacher who was having trouble with her class. One little boy, Billy, refused to go with the rest of the children to have his milk at break time. When the teacher went over to the little lad he told her, 'Bugger off.'

The first time this happened, the teacher decided to turn a deaf ear, but when he said the same thing the next day, she scolded him, 'Don't you ever let me hear you say that again.'

But sure enough, the next morning, the same thing happened. Billy refused to take his milk and told the teacher, 'Bugger you and your milk.'

Fed up with the lad's rudeness, she finally called Billy's mum in to witness his behaviour. Once more Billy refused to drink the milk and said to the teacher, 'Bugger you and your milk.'

'Well, then,' said the teacher to his mother, 'what do you think of that?'

'Simple,' replied Billy's mum. 'Bugger him – don't give the little shit any milk.'

Glynnis looked puzzled as sports-mad Bert watched the nail-biting finish of the one-day cricket final. 'I can't understand it,' she said. 'I thought they had decided who was the best team *last* year.'

A sexy young wife had just got out of the bath when the doorbell rang. Somewhat nervously she called out, 'Hello, who is it?'

'Good-day, madam,' came the reply. 'It's the blind man.'

Reassured, she threw open the front door stark naked and found herself confronted by a workman very obviously staring at her gorgeous body.

'Good morning, madam,' he repeated with a broad smile. 'Where do you want me to put your blinds?'

A middle-aged couple were lying in bed. They hadn't made love for several weeks, but the man was beginning to feel a bit randy and asked, 'How about taking your dressing-gown off, darling?'

However, his wife was unimpressed. So he tried again. 'Go on,' he said, 'take off your dressing-gown. We haven't done it for ages.'

'No,' said his wife, turning away from him.

This went on for several minutes until they were interrupted by the cat wailing to be let out. The husband got out of bed, went and saw to the cat, and returned to the bedroom to find the door locked. Infuriated, he cried out, 'Let me in or I'll break the door down.'

'Tell me another,' retorted his wife. 'You couldn't even get my dressing-gown off.'

My wife refused to breast-feed her baby. Said it hurt too much when she boiled the nipples.

You know, I came across a bloke whose wife had heard that nine out of ten accidents happen within five miles of the home. Now she wants to move!

Like many men, Sam, though himself experienced between the sheets, was desperate to marry a virgin. One day he was out in his car with Wendy, a likely candidate, when he pulled into a lay-by. Moving his hand to his flies, he said, 'Darling, would you like to see my . . . er . . . wee-wee?'

Wendy blushed and told him, 'No, please. Don't do that here.'

Smiling to himself at this reassuring news about her innocence, Sam proposed and was accepted.

On their wedding night Sam was lying on the bed when he unzipped himself and flopped his manhood out for Wendy to look at. 'It's not really a "wee-wee",' he explained. 'It's called a cock.'

'Huh,' replied Wendy contemptuously, 'call that a cock?'

A Northerner and his shy young bride were just about to enjoy their wedding night. She pointed to his balls and asked, 'What are those for?'

Bluntly he replied, 'They're just for show.'

Some minutes later he was happily working away inside, but his new partner, growing bolder by the minute, was clearly unfulfilled. Finally she whispered, 'Darling . . . we're just simple folk – put the show in as well.'

What's the definition of a test-tube baby? A womb with a view.

A bridegroom was desperately trying to satisfy his lusty young bride on their wedding night. 'More rope,' she gasped, 'more rope,' as he pumped away inside.

He obliged, but a few minutes later she was again urging, 'More rope, more rope.'

Once more the young man did his best, but seconds later she again gasped, 'More rope, darling, more rope.'

By this time the bridegroom was at a loss and in desperation he thrust his balls inside too.

To his dismay, his bride called out once again, 'More rope, more rope – and not so many of the knots next time!'

Dudley was complaining to Frank about his young daughter. 'She's got this thing about ashtrays,' he moaned. 'Wherever we go, she's always looking for one to empty. It's very embarrassing.'

'That's not so bad, is it?' said Frank. 'At least she's clean and tidy.'

'I know,' sighed Dudley, 'but sometimes she won't eat anything else at all.'

A midwife was comforting a woman who was just going into labour. 'Don't worry, Miss Jones,' she said. 'You'll have the baby in exactly the same position as you conceived it.'

'Help!' said the patient in alarm. 'They'll never fit all the doctors and nurses inside my boyfriend's mini!'

A bridegroom and his bride were going off into the night after their wedding reception. While he was driving, the husband moved his hand over and began stroking his bride's thighs in a sensual manner.

'Hey, cut that out,' shouted the bride. 'I'm a married woman now!'

The new au pair was explaining over the phone to the wife that things were going fine at home.

'I have bathed the children and put them to bed, ja,' she said. 'The only one who was any trouble was the big boy with the blond hair – he was very naughty!'

'Oh my God,' screamed the wife down the phone, 'that's my husband!'

A young wife was complaining to her mother, 'If I had known sex was like that I'd have never have married.'

'What's up? What does he make you do?' asked the mother.

'He wants me to make love every night,' sobbed the daughter.

'But's that quite normal,' explained her mother.

'But the way he wants me to do it – it's not decent!' wailed the younger woman.

'How does he make you do it?' asked the mother.

'With the lights on!' howled her daughter.

'You know, I bought my wife a lovely chair for her birthday,' Sid told his pal Alfie. 'But the rest of the family won't let me switch it on.'

PUSSIES GALORE

One of the best ways of shocking women is talking to them directly about sex.

'Oh, you do that? How could you do that, you dirty cows, and you all do it don't you?' I tell them in my shows and they fall about laughing. You get these girls in the audience sitting with their mums and cringing in embarrassment and you know they're saying, 'Oh don't, my mum's right next to me!'

They all do it, even the old ones, the seventy year olds. You can pick on them particularly. 'You dirty cows, you've flattened a bit of grass in your time haven't you?' I tell them. They love it.

Of course, they're out for a laugh when they come to my show. Most of them know me. I'm up on stage and it's all a question of timing to get them going. Black women are the best. They fall about laughing and scream the place down. American women do a lot of screaming too, but they're used to the sort of stand-up comedians who talk at them instead of to them. When I've been on stage in places like Las Vagas, I've to slow down my delivery so they can understand. But what really throws them is having someone on stage chatting to them directly – especially about sex. American comics work very blue, but when an audience has someone talking directly to them that's something else and with some of the gags like these you can see why.

What's the definition of a nymphomaniac? A woman who's more highly sexed than you.

Joe was vigorously screwing his new girlfriend.
'Please be gentle,' she begged. 'I've got a weak heart.'
'Don't worry,' Joe told her, 'when I get that far I'll slow down.'

There was a club for nymphomaniacs where all they did was sit round discussing prospective members.

Why does Nancy Reagan always sit on top? Because Ronnie can only screw up.

John was a polite young man desperate for a lay, so one night he arranged a blind date. To his horror he arrived at the girl's house and found that she was disabled and needed a wheelchair.

Being too polite just to run for it, John duly took her out for a drink followed by a meal. By this stage he was in a fix because the girl was very pretty but he couldn't see how he could get anywhere with her. But, as if she was reading his mind, she suggested they went to the local sports centre.

'I'll just hang from the top wall bar and you can fuck me,' she said. So John did just that and to his amazement the two of them had a great time, though they both got bruised and scratched in their passion.

When it was time to go home, John drove her up to the front door in some trepidation, wondering what her old man was going to say when he saw the state his daughter was in. And when her dad appeared, he started stammering, 'I ... I ... I'm sorry, sir ... I ... I ...'

'There's no need to apologize, lad,' interrupted the father, 'the last two bastards left the poor girl hanging there.'

Sophie had a bad pain in her arm and was desperate to see the doctor. She turned up at the surgery very early one morning and was pleased to see a smartly dressed young man there.

'I've got a bad pain in my arm,' she said to him, 'could you see to it?'

'OK,' he replied, 'just lie down and I'll see to it.'

A few minutes later Sophie shouted, 'Doctor, doctor – *that's* not my arm!'

'And neither am I the doctor,' the man replied with a grin.

A man was making love to his new woman for the first time. He did his best and worked away between her legs but absolutely failed to make her respond.

'I'm afraid it's your organ,' said the girl. 'It's not big enough.'

'Well,' snorted the man angrily, 'I'd no idea I was going to be playing in a cathedral!'

Betty went into a chemist's where the young man serving told her, 'Don't say anything – I can read minds. Let me guess what you want.' And he handed her a packet of Durex.

'Actually, I wanted some Andrex,' said Betty.

'Well, I didn't miss by much, did I?' said the shop assistant.

Sally was getting very frustrated with her new date. She'd taken the young hunk back to her place but he'd failed to respond to any of her moves. She'd tried kissing him, caressing his body, nibbling his ear and rubbing her breasts against him, but to no avail. He just sat there uncomfortably on the settee.

Getting annoyed, she exclaimed, 'Look, I've got a hole down there, you know.'

'Ah,' said the young man with relief, 'I wondered where the draught was coming from.'

What's better than four carnations on a piano? Tulips on an organ ...

A horny young girl was out with her athletic boyfriend who insisted on going ice-skating. The girl couldn't skate, but watched her bloke until he came over to her and put his frozen hands up her skirt.

'Hey, what did you do that for?' asked the girl.

'I'm sorry, it's just my hands get cold out there,' he told her.

This went on a few more times; each time he came over and put his hands up her skirt.

By the fifth time her boyfriend came back, the girl was getting very frustrated. 'Tell me,' she asked him hopefully, 'don't your ears ever got cold as well?'

Two bitchy women having a chat.

First woman: 'I must get home, I'm spending the weekend in bed with a man.'

Second woman: 'How nice – anyone you know?'

A man was told by his wife that he was a real animal lover. She said he screwed like a donkey.

A young woman from the town was stranded one night in the countryside miles from anywhere, except for a small hovel. She knocked at the door to find two real old countrymen living there. Eventually they allowed the woman to spend the night there, but only if she agreed to sleep with them. The woman sighed, but reluctantly accepted.

Before they got into bed she handed each of them a condom, saying, 'At least I won't get pregnant.'

The night passed and the woman left. A month later the two old boys were sitting downstairs recalling her visit.

''Ere, Bert,' said one of them, 'do you really care if that woman gets up the spout?'

'Can't say as I do,' said Bert.

'Well, in that case,' replied his friend, 'let's take these ruddy things off now.'

George was in his cellar late one night when he saw, to his astonishment, a little mouse raping a large rat. So he captured the little beast, took it upstairs and tried it on the cat. Sure enough, the rampant little mouse did the same to the Siamese, and not content with that did the family bull terrier for good measure. George was amazed and took the mouse upstairs to show his wife.

As soon as she clapped eyes on it, she started screaming and hid under the pillow.

'But, darling, listen to this ...' started George.

'For God's sake,' yelled his wife, interrupting, 'get that bloody sex maniac out of here!'

Why is spaghetti like a woman? They both squirm around when you get them ...

A woman decided to be a bit exotic and went to a tattooist. She asked for a tattoo of Paul Newman on the top of one thigh and a tattoo of Steve McQueen on the top of the other.

The tattooist laboured away and finally finished his work, but when the client looked at what he'd done, she was horrified and complained, 'These don't look anything like Paul Newman and Steve McQueen.'

This started a flaming row which only calmed down when they agreed to find a third person to judge the work independently. So they pulled in from the street the first person they found, who happened to be a drunk just reeling out of a pub.

The woman dropped her clothes and the tattoo artist said to the drunk, 'Isn't that the spitting image of Paul Newman?'

Getting down on hands and knees, the drunk peered closely, and said, 'I'm not sure.'

'How about this one – isn't that the spitting image of Steve McQueen?' asked the tattoo artist.

Again the drunk peered closely before saying, 'You know, I'm not sure.' Then he added, 'But this fellow in the middle with the beard and the bad breath – that's got to be Orson Welles.'

Little Red Riding Hood was strolling through the dark forest when the Big Bad Wolf jumped out. 'I'm going to eat you up,' he told the little girl.

'Just my luck,' said Little Red Riding Hood. 'Doesn't anyone screw any more?'

Josie was a bright town girl whose car broke down one night, forcing her to seek refuge in a farmhouse. Because there was no room in the house itself, the farmer told her she would have to spend the night in the same bed as his seventeen-year-old son, Tom, who slept in the barn. So he showed Josie out to the barn where they found Tom still wide awake.

'Why aren't you asleep?' asked his father.

'Because I haven't had my cocoa yet,' the boy replied.

Anyway, Josie stripped off, got in with the lad and started playing with him, arousing his impressive young manhood.

After a while she couldn't contain herself any longer and whispered in his ear, 'Now's your chance.'

So Tom got out of bed and drank his cocoa.

How do you make a bull work hard? Give him a tight jersey.

Samantha was picked up by a businessman one night. He was obviously very rich, but as they were getting undressed he turned out to be very fussy.

'That's a lot of wool,' he remarked as she took off her blouse to show her armpits.

Peeved at this, Samantha continued undressing and finally took off her knickers.

'God, that's a lot of wool,' exclaimed her lover.

'Listen,' she snapped, 'what do you want to do – screw or knit?'

What's the difference between a Rolls-Royce and Britt Ekland? Most people haven't been in a Rolls-Royce.

Did you hear about the woman who was banned from the hotel swimming pool after she was seen going down for the third time?

Robinson had been stranded on a desert island since he was a boy. All alone he had survived on a diet of just seaweed and clams. All he ever ate was seaweed and clams.

One day he saw a figure floating in the water and dashed into the waves just in time to rescue the most gorgeous blonde from drowning. Once she had recovered she wanted to show her thanks and offered Robinson the chance to sleep with her.

Robinson had to explain that he didn't know what sex was, so the blonde said that she would show him. After she had shown him several times in the surf she turned to Robinson and asked, 'Well, what do you think of sex?'

'Great,' he replied. 'But look what it did to my clam digger.'

Why are women like pianos? When they're not up-right, they're grand.

Mrs Smythe was having a shower one day when little Rupert burst in. 'Mummy, what's that?' he asked pointing at her thick bush of pubic hair. Embarrassed, she replied, 'That's my sponge.'

'That explains it,' said Rupert, 'because yesterday I saw the au pair washing Daddy's face with hers.'

An astronaut arrived on Mars and was confronted by the sight of a beautiful Martian woman stirring a boiling cauldron.

When he asked what she was doing, she replied, 'I'm making babies.'

'Really,' said the astronaut. 'We do it differently on earth.' To prove the point he whipped out his tool and gave her a good screw.

When he'd finished, the Martian woman said, 'Fine, but where's the baby?'

'It takes another nine earth months for it to come,' the astronaut explained.

'In that case,' said the Martian woman, pulling him back on her, 'why did you stop stirring?'

Why do women scratch their eyes in the morning? Because they've got no balls.

The stunning hitch-hiker got into Clem's car and coyly told him she was a witch.

'What do you mean?' he asked.

'I can turn you into anything I want,' replied the passenger.

And sure enough a few minutes later she undid the buttons on her blouse. And he turned into a layby.

The disciple one day followed his late master up to heaven and was delighted to see his former spiritual adviser languishing with a gorgeous leggy brunette.

'Master,' said the disciple, 'how good to see that you have been rewarded with what you so obviously deserve.'

'Reward, nothing,' snapped the old man. 'I'm her bloody punishment!'

Bimbo to a friend: 'I've never been so insulted in my life — I asked him to drive me straight home and he did.'

A middle-aged widow was spending the night in a seaside boarding-house. As she was the last to arrive there was hardly any room. The landlord gave her the blunt choice, 'You can sleep down here on the living-room floor or you can share a bed with the Kid – which you'd probably prefer.'

But the widow didn't much like children and decided to opt for the floor, where she spent a quiet but uncomfortable night. In the morning a hunky eighteen-year-old with a massive bulge in his jeans walked into the room.

'Who the hell are you?' asked the widow.

'They call me the Kid,' replied the youth. 'And who are you?'

'Oh, I'm just the half-wit who spent the night on the floor,' came the reply.

God must have been pissed when he made Woman — he put the ignition too close to the exhaust.

Graffiti seen in the dust on the back of a lorry: 'One Kate Bush is worth two in the hand.'

First woman: 'My husband spends so much time working away from home that when he comes back I don't recognize him any more.'
Second woman: 'How awful! What on earth do you do?'
First woman: 'Well, I go to bed with every man that calls – just in case.'

When she was asked her idea of perfect sexual foreplay, Kathy gave the example of a five-piece rock band whose members she knew.

'What do you mean?' asked her friend.

'It's simple,' said Kathy. 'Each of them takes it in turn to screw the arse off me while the other four play.'

An eccentric but very wealthy old gent was staying in a top penthouse one evening when he rang up a local escort agency and asked for the top girl they had. 'Money's no object,' he assured them. 'I'll pay her £500 for the night.'

Within half an hour there was a knock at his door and in walked Mandy, an exquisite-looking redhead.

'Hi,' she said to the old man, 'what would you like?'

The old man said he would like a bath, so Mandy ran the water, he stripped off and got in.

'Now what would you like?' asked Mandy soothingly.

'Make waves,' said the old gent.

So Mandy sat on the edge of the bath and made waves.

A few minutes later Mandy asked, 'Now what would you like me to do?'

'Thunder,' said the old buffer. 'Bang your hand against the wall.'

What do you call a beautiful girl in Birmingham? A tourist.

So Mandy banged the partition to make the sound of thunder.

This went on for a few more minutes when Mandy asked, 'Sir, what would you like me to do now?'

The old man replied, 'Lightning – make it flash in here.' So Mandy sat there making waves, thunder and switching the light on and off to make lightning. She kept this up for a few minutes more and then said to the old boy, exasperated, 'Excuse me, but I'm a very expensive and proficient prostitute. Don't you want sex?'

To which the old man replied, 'In this weather? You must must be joking.'

Why do Eskimo women get pregnant so often? Because their hands are too cold to get the condoms out of the packet.

How do you get a Scots girl pregnant? Sell her boyfriend a packet of Durex and tell him there's money back on the empties.

The king was off on a crusade, but was worried about leaving his attractive and randy young queen alone with the courtiers. He consulted with his advisers and decided to fit a small guillotine inside her fanny.

A long year passed and the king finally returned from his travels. The first thing he did was to line up ten courtiers and ask them who had slept with the queen. But no one admitted to laying her. The king didn't believe them, though, and ordered them, one at a time, to take their trousers down. One by one the courtiers obeyed and the king saw that each had lost his manhood because of the queen's guillotine. All except one that is.

So the king called in his guards and ordered the nine faithless courtiers to be executed. He then said to the tenth courtier who still had his penis, 'Well done. You alone have been faithful to your sovereign. Tell me, how can I reward you?'

'Nnnnn . . . nnnnn . . . nnnnn,' replied the courtier, struggling to talk without his tongue.

Desmond couldn't make up his mind which girl to go for, fat Lesley or cute Lucy. Finally he asked his mate Sid for advice. Sid looked at Des as if he was crazy. 'Desmond,' he said finally, 'you've gotta screw Luce!'

Do you know why female rabbits get pregnant so often? Ever seen what they do to French lettuce?

Why is a Page Three girl like a seat at a Lord's cricket ground? Both cause stiff members.

Did you hear about the athlete who gave up running and took to women after a friend told him that a miss was as good as a mile?

There was a young lady called Karen,
Who went out with a man called Sir Darren.
But she got quite a fright
When she visited her young knight
And found him in bed with a baron.

'My girlfriend's pretty dirty,' Len admitted to his mates, **'... and after a bath she's a real stunner.'**

Businessman: 'I want to send some information to my new girlfriend in Paris.'
Communications expert: 'Fax?'
Businessman: 'Like a bloody whore, man.'

A foreigner walked into a bar frequented by prostitutes thinking it was the type of café he was used to at home. ''Scuse me,' he stuttered in his poor English, 'how much Horlicks?'

'Depends how much you pay her,' replied the barmaid.

Two women were chatting in a dentist's waiting-room and got around to talking about sex.

'I never made love to my husband before we got married,' said one of them. 'How about you?'

'I don't know,' replied the other. 'What's his name?'

Joe was delighted when his teenage son passed his 'A' levels and rewarded him by giving him thirty quid. 'Take this down to the brothel, son. And have a good time,' said Joe proudly.

Later in the day he asked his boy how it had gone.

'It was marvellous, Dad,' said the lad. 'And I also managed to save thirty pounds.'

'That's amazing,' replied Joe. 'How did you manage to do that?'

'I went and screwed Granny instead.'

'You did what?' exploded Joe. 'You mean to say you screwed my mother?'

'Why not?' replied his son. 'You've been shafting mine for years!'

Jack was understandably self-conscious about his wooden leg and didn't even tell his girlfriend, randy Anne. One day he proposed and was on the verge of telling his intended about his little problem. But he chickened out and told her instead, 'I've got a bit of a surprise for you on our wedding night.' Anne flushed with pleasure at these words and answered, 'Darling – I can hardly wait.'

So the big day came. Everything went smoothly until Jack and Anne were alone together in the hotel bedroom. 'Now then,' said Anne seductively, 'what is it you were going to show me?' Jack blushed again, turned off the light, took off his trousers – and took off his two-foot long wooden leg and thrust it into Anne's hands.

'Christ!' she squealed with delight. 'Now, that's what I call a real surprise!'

A Polish nun was explaining to a young man her awful experiences in the last war. 'First when the Germans came, they burst into the convent and raped every nun except Sister Jo. And then when the Ukrainians came, ah! it was horrible also, they burst into the convent and raped every nun in the place except Sister Jo.' And the Polish nun continued, 'Then the Russians came and, Mother of Mercy, was that bad, they burst in and raped every single nun except Sister Jo.'

The young man was baffled. 'But tell me, why on earth didn't they rape Sister Jo?'

'Ah well,' said the Polish nun, 'I guess she wasn't in to that sort of thing.'

A peasant woman was bending over washing her clothes in the river one day when an army passed. Seeing their chance, many of the soldiers, who had not had a woman for months, came up behind her, lifted her skirts and gave her a good going over from the rear. The woman didn't bat an eyelid, didn't even turn round as soldiers took it in turns. Finally they had had their fill and were moving off when the regimental ram saw what had been happening and, feeling horny too, charged at the woman and thrust in his massive tool.

As the ram got off, the woman, who was still washing, called out, 'And will that last nice young man please leave his name and address!'

Zoe went to her priest for advice. 'Father, I've been walking out with this young man for a while now. On our first date he gave me a peck on the cheek. On the second date he kissed me on the lips and put his tongue inside my mouth. On the third time he fondled my breasts. Then on the fourth date he played with my pussy. And on the fifth he put ten inches up me.'

'What, pray child, is it you need to know?' asked the old priest.

'Just this, Father,' said Zoe, 'if I keep seeing him do you think there's a danger he will rape me?'

A shy young music student was out on his first date with a girl. Later she dragged him into the back of his car, but he proved very unresponsive despite her best efforts to kiss and cuddle him. Finally she leant over him and said, 'Hey, I don't think you quite get the idea ... I want to play with your "organ".'

So he pulled out his harmonica and handed it to her.

A stranger in town goes into a pub. After a while he sees a pretty young thing sitting on her own at the bar and sits down next to her. 'Excuse me, but would you like a drink?' he asks politely.

'What's that? You want to take me from behind?' she asks loudly.

Red-faced, he replied that he only wanted to buy her a drink.

'Oh – you do want to take me from behind,' says the girl, this time yelling at the top of her voice so the whole pub can hear.

Naturally enough the drinkers at the bar look menacingly at the stranger and he retires humiliated to a corner to sit on his own.

After a while, to his amazement, the girl comes over to him. 'I'm very sorry I did that to you,' she explained, 'but I'm studying psychology and doing an essay on how people react to embarrassment.'

The man yells, 'Fifty quid? Fifty quid just to take you from behind?'

A randy young girl was being thrown out of a posh nightclub for pestering some of the famous clients.

As the bouncer was leading her out, she made one last attempt at persuading him to let her stay. 'I've got an itchy pussy,' she said, slipping a hand into his trouser pocket.

'I don't care if you do drive a Japanese car – you've still got to get into it and drive away,' said the bouncer.

A shy young lad was out on his first date with the village tart. After a bit of clumsy kissing in a dark lane, the young man whispered, 'I'd love a little pussy right now,' and took out his modest manhood.

'So would I,' sighed the tart. 'Mine's as big as a bucket!'

What do you get after necking with Eskimo women? Frost bite.

A couple of guys were at a loose end in town one day. Murphy decided to pop into a church for confession.

'What for?' asked his mate. 'Absolution?'

'Never you mind,' said Paddy.

Inside the church he told the priest, 'Father, I have sinned. I have slept with one of the tarts in town.'

'That is indeed serious,' the priest replied. 'Now, tell me, was it Lucy Jones?'

Paddy answered, 'Father, in truth, I will not tell you who it was, but it was not Lucy Jones.'

'Was it Mandy Watts?'

'Father, I canot say who it was, but it was not Mandy Watts.'

'Well, was it Sue Smith?'

Again Paddy refused to say who it was but added that it wasn't Sue Smith.

'Well, I'm afraid if you won't tell me, there's nothing I can do for you,' the priest said finally. 'Now be on your way.'

So Paddy went back outside to be greeted by his sceptical friend who asked, 'Well, did you get forgiveness then?'

'No,' Paddy told him, 'but I got some red-hot tips.'

Two white women were exploring in Africa when they went past a river bank. There, to their astonishment, was a huge black man bathing with the biggest prick either of them had ever seen.

The two women went over to the man where he was bathing, and through an interpreter told him they were intrigued by the size of his apparatus.

'Huh!' came back the peeved reply. 'Does not the member of the white man also shrink in cold water?'

Did you hear about the woman who had an orgasm every time she sneezed? She went to the countryside one summer, caught hay fever and had a whale of a time.

Did you hear about the insurance salesman who did the business with a housewife because she wasn't adequately covered?

A guy was on a date with this girl for the first time. 'After a few drinks, you look a real smasher,' he told her.

'That's kind of you,' she cooed, 'but I haven't touched a drop.'

'No,' he said, 'but I have.'

SECRETARY BIRDS AND QUEEN BEES

I've nothing against women making a bob or two but there are some jobs they'll never be able to do. You don't see women bod carriers and I don't know how those girls who want to be miners are going to get on down the pit heaving the coal about. But if they want to have a go, let them. We've even got women wrestlers now, but we never see them fighting men. That would be good. Mind you, I read a couple of cases of men being battered by their wives so some poor devils are going to have to watch out from now on if they aren't careful.

In my line of business I don't think there are any really funny women stand-up comedians – certainly not over here anyway. Maybe that's because the British don't like women to be rude and brash. We accept acts like Dame Edna's, because deep down we know they're only men dressed up. That's why drag artists are funny. A lot of girls in show business these days do impressions and many of them are good at it, but there aren't any real comics in the true sense.

Most of the really funny wonen seem to be American too. I went to see Shirley Maclaine at the Victoria Palace, sitting in the front row. She came down into the audience to grab someone for a bit in her act and came to within two seats from me. Everybody in the wings and all the orchestra knew I was in the theatre that night, but she didn't know who I was and very nearly dragged me up on stage. I nearly died but luckily she stopped short and picked someone else. She was excellent. They really know how to do shows like that over in the States.

Among working women, policewomen are quite good fun

to have in an audience, in fact the police have generally got a good sense of humour, and when I ask if there are any watching the show and a policewoman owns up, I ask, 'Have you got batteries in your truncheon?' and things like that which they laugh at as loudly as everyone else.

Nurses are good too. You can never shock them because they've seen it all, giving people bed baths and everything – and some of the things you read about those bed baths makes it sound almost worth being ill!

I've always thought modelling's a very unfair career. Good models can earn £50 an hour ... but bad ones can make a lot more.

A group of civilian secretaries were flown down to the Falklands to help with a backlog of paperwork. After they landed, the army major who met them warned them to watch out for his men 'who hadn't seen a woman in months'.

'Don't worry,' replied one of the super secs, tapping her forehead. 'We've got it up here.'

'It doesn't matter where you've got it,' snapped the major. 'My lot will bloody well find it.'

Did you hear about the woman racing driver who came last in the Grand Prix? She kept having to stop in the pits to ask the way ...

Young Miss Smith was having trouble getting her class to understand the use of the word 'certainly'. She asked them to give a few examples. Jimmy said, 'Apples are certainly green.'

'That's all right,' said Miss Smith, 'but they can also be red.'

Susie said, 'Bananas are certainly yellow.'

'Good,' said Miss Smith, growing exasperated, 'but they can also be green. Can anyone give me a real use of the word?'

Just then little Joe stuck up his hand and asked, 'Miss, can you tell me, do farts have lumps in them?'

Horrified, she replied, 'How dare you be so rude. Of course they don't have lumps.'

'In that case,' said Joe triumphantly, 'I have most certainly shat in my pants.'

There was a butcher who opened a new shop and offered his first ten women customers a free goose.

A middle-aged prostitute who had slept with literally thousands of men finally collapsed and died one night as she was in the middle of another torrid session with a regular client.

As her soul floated up to heaven she was met by a very impressive man with a large helmet and axe. 'Welcome, madam,' he boomed, 'I am Thor.'

'Tho am I, honey,' sighed the prostitute, 'tho am I.'

Why did the army make their women paratroopers wear jock straps? So they couldn't whistle on the way down.

Stunning brunette Sophie was a struggling model who was determined to gatecrash a fancy-dress ball to meet celebrities. Unfortunately she had no money to hire a costume and turned up stark naked except for black shoes and black gloves.

'I'm sorry,' said the bouncer sniffily. 'You can't come in. You don't represent anything.'

'Of course I do,' said Sophie. 'I'm the Five of Spades.'

Did you hear about the girl who works in the hat factory? She gets felt five times a day. Or her friend in the mining business who keeps getting shafted?

A rich, shrewish housewife turned to her au pair one day and said, 'You know, I'm sure my husband is having it off with his secretary.'

'Forget it,' replied the au pair, 'I know you're just trying to make me jealous.'

As the prostitute said to her client, 'It's a real business doing pleasure with you.'

Did you hear about the prostitute who decided to insure each of her legs for a million pounds? She said between the two of them she made a very good living.

Sue, a girl of experience, was trying to seduce a well-built farmer's son in a hay loft but without much success because the poor lad was a complete innocent. In the end she gave him ten pounds so they could 'play a game' and soon she had the confused lad, his massive manhood fully aroused, on top and in position.

'Right' said Sue. 'Now go in, now out, now in again, now out ...'

But the baffled lad tore himself off and glared at Sue. 'You can keep your ten quid,' he stormed. 'You just can't make up your mind what you want, can you?'

Three nuns were going in for confession. The first said, 'Forgive me. I have sinned. I let my finger touch a man's penis.'

The priest replied, 'Say twelve Hail Marys and then put your finger in this holy water.'

The second nun said, 'Forgive me, Father, for I have sinned. I allowed my hand to touch a man's penis.'

The priest told her, 'Say twelve Hail Marys and douse your hand in this holy water.'

And the third nun said rather croakily, 'Forgive me, Father ... er, I feel rather thirsty.'

An ageing businessman called Jerry was very pleased with himself when he managed to pick up a pretty young student at a party and take her off for a night's bonking. In the morning the girl turned to him and said, 'How about twenty pounds for last night?'

Amazed, Jerry replied, 'You're a prostitute? But I thought you were a student?'

'So I am,' replied the girl. 'I'm doing a course in business studies.'

What's the difference between a priest praying and a nun in the bath? The priest has hope in his soul.

Flouncy blonde: 'Is this dress too low cut?'
Shop assistant: 'Madam, do you have hairs on your chest?'
Flouncy blonde: 'Of course not.'
Shop assistant: 'In that case it's too low cut.'

Hollywood is the city of dreams ... where young actresses flock to make love beneath the stars.

A man rushes into a bar muttering something under his breath and immediately orders a double vodka, followed by another. After several more rounds of the same the barman asks the man, pretty pissed by now, what the matter is. The man looks up and asks, 'Tell me, how big is a penguin?'

'Well, they're about two feet tall,' replied the barman. 'But why do you want to know?'

'Bloody hell,' said the man ordering another drink. 'In that case I think I've just run over a nun.'

Did you hear about the woman lawyer who was caught with no briefs? She was accused of being a solicitor.

A young actress is going for a big interview with a powerful film director. As she walks into the outer office his kindly secretary looks up and says, 'Listen. I must warn you – if the boss gets you alone in there he'll more than likely rip your dress right off you.'

'Thanks for the warning,' said the actress, hastily departing. 'I'd better go and put on an old dress.'

Film ratings:
U – the good guy gets the girl
PG – the bad guy gets the girl
18 – everybody gets the girl

Why are whores and margarine the same? They both spread for bread.

A top star of porn videos has just quit, claiming she doesn't like many of the parts she's asked to play with ...

A burly lorry driver on a trip abroad went to visit a brothel in Germany. He asked the madame if he could have the biggest, toughest woman in the place to satisfy his needs.

He was shown into a room and pretty soon this massive fraulein walked in, stark naked, carrying a few bottles of beer. The burly driver was quickly aroused by the sight of this huge woman and was even more turned on when the prostitute immediately got down on all fours and thrust her fanny into the air.

'You're really into hard sex, aren't you?' said the lorry driver admiringly.

'Sex?' replied the woman, 'I just thought you'd like to open the beer first ...'

A young woman snuggled up to Bert in a bar. 'I'm yours for the asking,' she murmured, ' ... and I'm asking thirty quid.'

What do you call a desert prostitute? A dry hump.

How do you make a hormone? Refuse to pay.

An airline pilot had just finished welcoming the passengers over the intercom but forgot to turn off the microphone when he turned to the co-pilot and said, in the full hearing of all the passengers, 'Right, John, I'll just have a coffee and then go and lay that new redhead in the cabin staff.'

The stewardess in question blushed bright red and rushed down the aisle to turn off the mike.

'There's no need to rush,' said a kindly old lady, as the stewardess hurried past her, 'the captain said he'd have a coffee first.'

A nun complained to her Mother Superior about the blue language of the Irish navvies digging a trench outside her room.

'There's nothing wrong with them,' said the Mother Superior. 'They're just ordinary folk who call a spade a spade.'

'No they don't,' snapped the nun. 'They call it a bleeding shovel.'

A young novice teacher was having terrible trouble getting her class to understand the basics of English. In particular one Swiss girl was very thick and instead of saying, 'I'm not hungry,' she kept repeating, 'I no angry.'

Patiently the teacher kept trying to get the same point across, but eventually, after two weeks the girl made the same mistake and the teacher exploded. 'For goodness sake,' she yelled, 'what do you mean "I no angry?"'

'Huh,' said the Swiss girl, 'you could have fooled me.'

No one would say that Lindsey was a bad driver ... but she still thinks she has to open the door to let the clutch out.

Graffitti on a church wall: 'It's OK to show a nun a little affection now and then — but don't get into the habit.'

Sister Margaret was determined to meet the Pope before she died and set off to Rome to see if she could catch a glimpse of him.

The nun joined the thousands of pilgrims who packed into St Peter's Square to see the Pope and thought to herself, 'This is hopeless. To be sure, the place is so full, I'll never get to meet the Pope.'

Just at that moment an extraordinary thing happened. The Pope stepped forward and out of the thousands of people there singled out a black nun in the crowds and walked over to her. The adoring masses watched in awe as he approached the black nun, leaned over and whispered something in her ear, then made the sign of the cross before returning to his spot.

Sister Margaret watched all of this spell-bound and it gave her an idea. 'I know,' she thought, 'I'll dress up like that black nun and the Pope is sure to pick me out too.'

So the next morning she got out the boot polish, blacked herself up and went into St Peter's Square to join the pilgrims. Sure enough the Pope was there and soon spotted Sister Margaret, the only black face in the crowd. Slowly he made his way towards her and she prayed, 'Oh Lord, thank you, thank you for this.'

The Pope came very close to her and in an ecstasy she saw him leaning over to her and heard him whisper, 'Hey nigger – I thought I told you yesterday to get the hell out of town.'

Flustered manageress to hunky but idle young male assistant: 'If you don't back your ideas up I'm going to have to suck you.'

A middle-aged woman went into the men's clothing department of a large department store and said to the young assistant, 'I want to change my husband's underpants which I bought here yesterday.'

'Of course, madam,' said the assistant, 'but what exactly's wrong with them?'

'You know Westminster Abbey?' asked the woman.

'Well, yes,' replied the puzzled girl.

'And the ballroom there?'

'But there is no ballroom,' said the assistant.

'That's exactly what my husband says about these pants.'

Miss Jones, an innocent young teacher, was asking her class what people did in different jobs.

'What do you think a doctor does?' she asked little Frances.

'My mummy says he cures people,' was the reply.

'That's right,' said Miss Jones. 'Jane, what do you think a pilot does?'

Jane answered, 'My daddy says he flies an aeroplane.'

Miss Jones said, 'Fine. Now it's your turn, Sally. What do you think secretaries do?'

Sally thought for a moment, then she said slowly, 'Well, according to what my uncle says, they go at it like rabbits.'

Did you hear about the randy woman jockey who decided to quit because she wasn't getting enough rides?

Peeved boss to his secretary: 'Tell me, Josephine, how is it that anybody can get so many things wrong in one day?'
Josephine: 'Easy – I get up early!'

Why did the prostitute refuse to serve the huge black man? Because he had one over the eight.

What's the difference between a male and female golfer? A hole-in-one.

A man had been waiting for ages for his lunch to be served. Finally he couldn't stand it any longer. 'Look here,' he yelled to the waitress, 'have I got to sit here until I starve?'

'Oh no,' said the waitress, 'we close in ten minutes.'

Where are the most prostitutes in the world? Lahore.

A self-employed businessman was going through a financial crisis. Talking to his secretary, Felicity, he said, 'It's got to the stage where the bank is sending back our cheques.'

'Oh,' she gushed, 'isn't that sweet of them.'

Tourist: 'There's a funny smell in this room – are you sure it's clean?'

Landlady: 'Of course it is. I washed all the linen myself. Look, feel the sheets; they're still a little damp.'

Did you hear about the prostitute who finally retired from the leper colony? Work kept dropping off.

A young prostitute had just returned earlier than expected from a 'tour of duty' in the Falklands, vowing she would never go back there.

'What's the matter?' asked a colleague. 'Wasn't there any work?'

'Oh, there's plenty of work all right,' she replied. 'I just got fed up with kneeling down on damp grass all day long with nothing on but a sheepskin coat.'

Frank married his secretary, Tessa, and while they were away on their honeymoon in Corfu, a Miss Bryant took Tessa's place in the busy office.

When Frank returned to work a colleague tried to introduce him to Miss Bryant, but he replied, 'There's no need for that. Miss Bryant and I already know each other. She stood in for Tessa on our honeymoon.'

A young executive was moaning to a mate about the girls in his office. 'They had a sit-down strike for a fortnight last month,' he grumbled.

'A fortnight?' asked his friend. 'Why did it take that long to sort out?'

'Sort out?' replied the executive laughing. 'It took us that long to notice they weren't working.'

Mother Superior sternly gathered together all her nuns to give them a good talking-to.

'I have some grave news,' she announced. 'A condom has been found in the convent.' Hearing this, ninety-nine nuns gasped in horror ... but one nun at the back went 'tee-hee'. 'What is more,' continued Mother Superior, 'the condom has been used.'

Again ninety-nine nuns gasped in horror – while one at the back went 'tee-hee'.

'But what I really have to tell you,' concluded the Mother Superior, 'is that the condom has a hole in the end,' at which point ninety-nuns roared with laughter as Sister Emmanuel fainted with shock.

Did you hear about the girl who left the brothel down the road? She was seeking a better paid position.

Timothy and Greg were out for a drink one night at their local. After a while Timothy asked Greg why he was so down. 'You've got a face like a wet weekend, mate,' he said.

Greg replied, 'So would you in my place. Since my girlfriend became a W-pc she says she's knackered most of the time and she's cut down our love-making to twice a week.'

'You think you've got problems,' said Timothy. 'She's cut me out altogether.'

Head office received a brief note from a branch manager, 'Request permission to grant Miss Jones maternity leave.'

The note was returned with the comment, 'We think your secretary made a little mistake.'

The branch manager returned his original note adding, 'Yes, she certainly did.'

Maureen's sister, a nun, fell ill while visiting a convent in Florida and had to be given special hospital treatment. After a couple of weeks the Mother Superior at the convent in Florida phoned Maureen with the good news that her sister was OK. There was now just the small question of the $50,000 hospital bill.

Maureen went up the wall. 'The stupid bitch,' she yelled down the phone. 'Our family can't afford to pay that!'

The Mother Superior was deeply offended. 'Your sister deserves more respect,' she said snootily. 'As a nun she is a bride of the Son of God.'

'In that case send the bloody bill to the father-in-law,' snapped Maureen.

A young woman got a job as a debt collector for a company selling household fittings. One of her first calls was to a bachelor flat. 'Mr Jones,' she began when her client opened the door, 'how about the next instalment on that carpet?'

'Great,' replied Mr Jones. 'It's better than paying for it.'

A cunning woman selling cosmetics door-to-door found it hard going in an up-market district until she came up with a brainwave. At the next house she said to the well-groomed woman who answered the door, 'Excuse me, madam, I don't really suppose you'd be interested in this new range of lipsticks. The lady opposite said it would be too expensive for you.'

There was the Dublin call-girl on her first trip out to do a blow job. She nearly electrocuted the poor guy with a hair-drier.

A middle-aged woman went to her lady GP and explained that she'd been feeling off-colour all week. Having examined the woman thoroughly, the doctor told her, 'I can't find anything wrong with you at all – it must be nervous tension.'

'OK, doctor,' replied the patient. 'I'll come back next week when you've calmed down a bit.'

First man: 'There are some great tarts down at the new brothel. One of them does a wonderful thing on a bed of ice.'
Second man: 'Bed of ice? What's that like, then?'
First man: 'Fantastic! But there's only one problem . . .'
Second man: 'What's that?'
First man: 'I think I caught a touch of whore frost.'

Did you hear about the book-keeper's widow? She'd let anyone make an entry now.

I suppose the similarity between a poultry breeder and a prostitute is that both raise cocks for a living.

The prostitute who was feeling a bit run down went to the chemist's to get some pills ... they soon had her back on her back.

Young Patricia had been out of work for some time and finally got a job doing nights with a firm of wholesalers. When she phoned her mum about it, however, the older woman got suspicious about the hours, and asked her daughter where exactly she would be working. When she heard, she blew her top.

'No, Mum!' shouted Patricia down the phone. 'I said ware-house, *ware*house!'

Did you know about the girl who had a funny act down at the local working men's club? She used to come on stage smothered in Dulux white emulsion. Called herself a paint stripper.

The Mother Superior of a top convent, sworn to a life of celibacy and freedom from sin, received some awful news. Her spiritual advisers told her that they had received visions and messages from on high that unless she made love to a man a terrible curse would fall on the convent and the world outside.

The Mother Superior was stunned and at first refused to have anything to do with the idea. But for several days her spiritual advisers told her that there was no choice. The message was clear, she had to submit herself for the sake of the world. Well, the Mother Superior thought about it deeply and finally told her advisers she would do it – but only on three conditions.

'What are they?' she was asked.

'The first is that the man in question must be dumb, so he can never speak of what he has done.'

'And the second?'

'The second condition is that the man must be blind, so that he may never recognize me again.'

There was a long pause. 'And the third condition?' they asked.

'He must have a big cock.'

A madame turned down a request from four new prostitutes to join her establishment.

'I've got enough girls already,' she explained, 'and I always think that too many hookers spoil the brothel.'

Avon lady to friend: **'I only got three orders this week.'**
Friend: **'What were they?'**
Avon lady: **'Get out, keep out – and don't come back!'**

A rather innocent foreign princess was being shown round a sperm bank. As she walked round a nurse was trying to explain, as delicately as possible, how the system worked. But to the nurse's horror, the princess insisted on looking inside the row of cubicles they were passing.

In the first the princess saw a little man who was self-consciously wanking himself off into a small plastic container.

'What's he doing that for?' asked the princess.

The nurse replied, 'He's just opened an account with us – and that's his first deposit.'

In the second cubicle the princess saw another man quite happily tossing himself off into a plastic bowl.

'And what's he doing?' asked the princess.

'He's a regular,' replied the nurse, 'who's been with us some time and is just building up his account.'

Then the princess looked into the third cubicle where she was amazed to see a woman energetically jerking her partner off into a bucket on the floor.

'What on earth are they doing?' exclaimed the princess.

'Oh,' replied the nurse, 'they're just trying to pay off their overdraft.'

There was the estate agent's secretary who was known for giving a good time ... you told her which place you liked and she showed it to you.

A not very well-endowed man rolled off from a big prostitute and asked, 'How did that compare with being screwed by my mate Big Jack?'

'There wasn't much in it,' she replied.

Then there was the secretary who had been at the job so long she was up to 30 mistakes a minute in her typing.

A young secretary was being interviewed for a new job.

'I'll be honest,' she said. 'I like the job you're offering but the last one I had gave more pay, had longer holidays and much better expenses.'

'So why did you leave?' asked the interviewer.

'The firm went bust.'

Hear about the laundryman who was booted out of a convent for asking if they had any dirty habits?

A boss was ticking off his secretary for laziness. 'Look, you never answer the phone any more – what's got into you?'

'I just got fed up,' replied his secretary, trimming her nails. 'It was nearly always for you.'

Did you hear about the boss with the urgent meeting who told his secretary he was going to be incommunicado? She asked for a contact number there ...

Or the bimbo whose boss said punctuation was the most important thing ... so she always arrived early for work?

Two secretaries were discussing work and one said to the other, 'I'm a bit worried that my boss may be getting interested in me.'

'What makes you think that?' asked her friend.

'He got the company doctor to put me on the pill today,' replied the other.

The boss was interviewing a new typist and asked, 'How good are you on the typewriter?'

'OK,' she said, 'but I'm better on the table.'

A meticulous boss at an accountancy firm was telling his new secretary, Daphne, about the standards he expected. 'Remember, I want you to check any figures at least four times before you give them to me.'

Later that day Daphne walked into the boss's office with a sheet of papers. 'I've checked those figures you wanted five times,' she said.

'Great, give them here,' said her boss.

' ... And here are the five different answers I got ...' continued Daphne.

A secretary is someone you pay to learn to type while she hunts for a husband.

A company executive was waiting for an important business call from overseas but had to shoot out for half-an-hour for an urgent appointment. When he got back he asked his secretary if anyone had phoned.

'Just one person – and she was a nutter.'

'How do you mean?' asked the boss.

'Well, this woman rang up and said, "Long distance from Tokyo to London",' replied his secretary. 'So I just said, "Of course it bloody is!" and put the phone down.'

First typist: **'How do you put down sex on expenses?'**
Second typist: **'Lunch.'**

Josie and Diana were struggling away typing awkwardly with the new hi-tech machines. 'Of course,' said Josie loudly so the whole office could hear, 'I don't really need to do this. I once had a beach house, unlimited supplies of fur coats and a sports car.'

Diana, also typing two-fingered, said, 'Me neither. I once had a cottage in the country, was flown all over the world and had a yacht.'

At this super sec Joan who had been sitting in the corner could bear no more. 'Listen, girls, I've also done a bit of whoring on the side – but where did you two bums learn to type?'

Sexy Sue the secretary had worked for five years in a small country office of a firm when she was promoted to work in the London office.

On her first day she arrived in her very best outfit, newly bought, to be told her job.

'Well,' said the boss, 'I think you can take it you'll be doing exactly the same sort of work as you were doing down in the country.'

'That's what I thought,' said Sue, slipping out of her clothes. 'Do you mind if I hang up my suit first?'

Did you hear about the legal secretary who was very good with briefs? She had her boss's down in seconds.

OLD
TROUTS
AND
DRAGONS

The history of comedy is filled with jokes about mothers-in-law. It was Les Dawson who told the first I remember hearing, when he said, 'My mother-in-law's here. She looks like a bulldog chewing a wasp.'

Once on the television I told a horrible mother-in-law joke but said just ahead of it, 'Before you start to sue me, mother-in-law, I'm talking about one of the other ones!'

Old women in general are funny. No one dares laugh at old women. You're not supposed to make fun of them. They're sacred. It's the same as when Harold Steptoe gets hold of Albert and wrings his neck. That always gets a laugh because there are times when everybody feels like doing the same thing but we don't, because we all have to be nice to old people.

I often pick out old women in an audience and have a laugh with them, asking things like, 'Why do you old girls always sit on deck chairs with your legs open and so people can see right up your skirt?' They don't always like that but everyone else falls about.

A middle-aged couple had a very dull sex life and realized they ought to do something to spice it up a little, so they bought a couple of sex manuals and read them together.

'Listen here,' said Fred, 'it says that when the man comes the woman should moan to give added excitement and pleasure. Shall we try that?'

'Sure,' said Ethel. 'Anything that will work. Let's do it tomorrow night.'

So they agreed that they were both going to make a special effort and as the evening arrived they were both very nice to each other, got undressed and climbed into bed. As usual Fred climbed on top and was soon inside Ethel.

'Do you want me to moan yet?' she asked.

'No, it's too soon for the moaning, I'll tell you when.'

So they continued for a few more minutes and Ethel asked again, 'Do you want me to moan yet, Fred?'

'No ...no ...it's too soon,' said Fred breathlessly. 'I'll tell you when to.'

They continued for a few more minutes and then Fred started panting fast. 'Now Ethel, now, start moaning!' he gasped.

And Ethel said, 'Well, I've just had an awful day, this morning the washing-machine broke down and then ...'

Bessie was a horny middle-aged woman who agreed to look after her neighbours' thirteen-year-old son while his parents were away. One night there was a thunderstorm and she persuaded him that she ought to sleep in his bed to make sure that he was all right.

After a while she said she wanted to swap sides and suggested they roll over each other.

'No need,' said the boy. 'I'll get out and walk round.'

A couple of minutes later Bessie tried the same ruse again, but again the boy got out and walked round.

This happened twice more before a frustrated Bessie exclaimed, 'Look, lad, you really don't know what I want, do you?'

'Of course I do,' said the boy. 'But there's no way you're going to get the whole bed!'

You can tell when your mother-in-law is staying as soon as you get inside the house. She parks her broomstick in the umbrella stand.

A blue-rinsed middle-aged woman decided it was time for a check-up with a top consultant.

He examined her thoroughly from top to toe, inside and out. Once he'd finished, he told her, 'You'll be glad to know that you've got the cleanest vagina I have ever seen.'

'So it should be,' said the patient. 'I have a coloured man who comes in and does for me three times a week.'

The old trout was being driven home late at night by a cabbie. As he was about to drop her off she confessed to him that she didn't have any money to pay him. As he came round to the back to have words with her, she promptly dropped her knickers and hitched up her skirt so that everything was in view, making it clear how she intended to pay.

'Oh Christ!' moaned the cabbie, 'don't you have anything smaller?'

An old lady in a restaurant noticed that a man at the next table was sitting with his flies open and his massive tool flopping out impressively on his lap.

Quickly she beckoned the waiter and hastily sent a note to the man. Astonished, the diner read, 'Sir, you are a disgrace, sitting at a table with your flies open like that.

'PS – here's my phone number.'

The mother-in-law of a mate of mine was so desperate for a man, she walked into her local with her pet dog and offered to sleep with anyone who could guess its age.

'Two hundred years old,' shouted a wag.

'Close enough,' replied the mother-in-law.

A bridegroom was getting undressed on his wedding night but couldn't remove his boots. He and his bride tried and tried, but he couldn't budge them. Eventually the bridegroom said, 'Looks like we'll have to use a knife.'

His mother-in-law, listening outside the door, screamed, 'No, no, Vaseline will do the trick!'

'You know,' said Alf to Barry, 'my mother-in-law always says she's going to dance on my grave. But I haven't told her yet that I'm going to be buried at sea.'

To celebrate their diamond wedding anniversary an elderly couple went to stay in a top London hotel. It was very romantic. On the first day the husband wined and dined his wife, took her up to their room with its splendid views, undressed and got into bed.

When the light was out he turned over, squeezed his wife's hand and said, 'Good night, darling.'

'Good night, dear,' she replied.

The next day they had another good time, a trip down the Thames, again followed by dinner. Once more they went to bed and once again the husband reached over and squeezed his wife's hand as he wished her good night.

Anyway, come the third day the elderly pair went sightseeing again, had dinner and prepared for bed feeling quite tired. Again the husband reached over towards his wife.

'Not tonight, dear,' she told him, 'I've got a headache.'

Mixed feelings are when you see your mother-in-law about to drive over a cliff ... in your brand-new BMW.

A young city slicker was watching a pretty milkmaid milking a cow in a field when in the distance he suddenly saw a bull charging towards them. To his astonishment the milkmaid stayed put and carried on calmly milking. Even more amazing the bull stopped dead in its tracks, took one look at the cow, turned round and sauntered back to its own patch.

'Why weren't you afraid?' asked the city slicker.

'There's no danger,' said the milkmaid. 'The bull was more frightened than you. This cow is his mother-in-law.'

My mate's mother-in-law speaks through her nose. She hasn't got any choice ... she's worn her mouth out.

Old Mrs Scrubit was boasting to her neighbour that she was ninety-three and had never needed to use glasses.

'No,' said her son-in-law to his mates as they slipped out to the boozer, 'she's always taken it straight from the bottle.'

A television viewer asked an ageing movie star, 'How many husbands have you had?'
'Including my own?' she replied.

An old woman, nearly blind with age, was being pushed in her wheelchair by a nurse round the grounds of a nursing home. Suddenly they surprised a young couple lying naked in the undergrowth with the man pumping away on top of the woman. Blushing deeply, they quickly gathered their clothes and ran off.

'I say, what were they doing?' asked the old woman.

'They were making love, madam,' said the nurse.

'Oh really . . .does that still go on?'

Way back in the Dark Ages there was an old woman living with her pretty young granddaughter in an English town that was constantly being invaded by the Vikings. These raids always took the same form: the Vikings burned down houses, looted them and raped any woman they chose.

One day another Viking raiding party smashed their way in, set fire to the buildings, stole all the valuables and started hunting for the women. One big Viking broke into the old woman's house and was about to rape her when the granddaughter rushed out from the corner where she had been hiding and bravely said, 'Spare my grandmother and take me instead.'

So the Viking raped the girl and left the old woman alone.

A few minutes later a second Viking broke in. The same thing happened. He started to molest the old woman, but her granddaughter again stepped out, said bravely, 'Spare my gran and take me instead,' and was duly raped.

Then a third Viking stormed in. He saw the old woman, made a move towards her when the young girl rushed out. But before she could say anything, her gran called out, 'Hush child, hush – after all a Viking raid is a Viking raid.'

Bert couldn't think why his mother-in-law was angry with him. The night before she'd come home and he'd told her, 'You've had your hair done. It looks much better.'

'No, I haven't,' replied his mother-in-law angrily. 'I've just been run over.'

Why do Italians grow moustaches? So they can look like their grandmothers.

An old bag who was late putting out her rubbish rushed out with her plastic sack when she heard the dustmen on the other side of the street and yelled at them, 'Am I too late?'

'No, madam,' one of them shouted back, 'hop in.'

Drunk to a pal at the bar: 'I left my wife over another woman.'
Friend: 'Really? Who?'
Drunk: 'Her mother.'

What's the difference between an Italian grandmother and an elephant?
Twenty pounds and a black dress.

A middle-aged woman whose looks were fast fading was walking out of a store when she heard a man's voice behind her.

'Excuse me,' gasped the man, who was laden down with shopping, 'but could you please open my car boot for me? I can't manage like this.'

'Certainly not, you might rape me,' said the woman.

'Don't be absurd,' said the man, 'how could I rape you carrying all this?'

'Well,' said the woman, 'you could put that bag down there, put another under your arm, lean one against the car and . . .'

Two elderly spinsters were talking and one confided to the other, 'The worst experience of my life was when my mother caught me playing with myself.'

'But that's happened to everyone in their life,' replied her companion.

'Yes . . .but it only happened last week.'

Man at a bar: 'I have to say it, but my mother-in-law is an angel.'
Companion: 'I wish mine was – but she's still alive.'

A couple were taking his mother-in-law on safari through a jungle. Suddenly the husband and wife saw the old woman standing in a clearing with a massive man-eating lion growling in front of her.

'For God's sake do something!' screamed the wife.

'No way,' said her husband, 'the lion got himself into this mess – he can get himself out of it.'

I heard of a bloke whose mother-in-law was so ugly that when she went to the zoo she had to buy two tickets – one to get in, the other to get out again.

'We've found a good way to get rid of mice in our house,' Barry told his mates during their tea-break. 'We invite my mother-in-law round to tea. When they see her coming, the mice throw themselves into the traps.'

A young man was taking his partially deaf brother back home by train when they got talking to a massive black man in their compartment. He told them he was going to Southend.

'What's that?' asked the deaf man.

'He says he's going to Southend, like us,' replied his brother, before asking the black man, 'Tell me, why are you going there?'

The black man replied that he was going to see his girlfriend.

'What's that?' asked the deaf man.

'He says he's going to see his girlfriend,' said his brother. 'She must be some woman,' he told the black man, 'to bring you out all this way.'

And the black man explained, 'Yes, she's got massive boobs, a great fanny, loves bondage and sucking me off.'

'What's that?' asked the deaf man.

'He says he knows mother,' replied his brother.

What's the definition of bad taste? When your grand-mother kisses you goodnight ...and slips her tongue inside your mouth.

A harassed young golfer was teeing off at the first hole and taking a very long time over it. Finally his companion asked him what the trouble was.

'My mother-in-law is visiting the clubhouse today,' he explained, 'and I want to make this a very good shot.'

'Don't be absurd,' said his partner. 'You'll never hit her from here.'

A Buddhist monk, a cardinal in the Catholic church and a Protestant bishop were travelling by car one day to a top-level religious conference.

Suddenly, to their horror, they saw in the rear-view mirror the Devil chasing down the road after them. Quickly they debated what they should do. The cardinal said he would write some lines of powerful prayer on a piece of paper and drop them out of the window for the Devil to read.

So he threw out the message and sure enough the Devil stopped to pick it up.

However, to their dismay, he threw it away after he had read it and continued after the three clerics in hot pursuit.

After a while, the Buddhist monk decided he'd write a few words from his ancient scriptures to see whether that would do the trick.

Again he dropped this out of the window and again the Devil stopped to pick it up.

But once more Old Nick carried on undeterred, continuing the chase.

By this stage he was gaining on the car and inside panic had taken over.

Finally the Protestant bishop decided to try a note, so he scribbled on a piece of paper and threw this out of the window.

The three clerics watched as the Devil picked up the paper, read the message and with a look of horror on his face turned tail and fled.

'Brilliant!' said the cardinal. 'What on earth did you say to make him go?' asked the monk.

'Easy,' replied the bishop, 'I just told him that very shortly we'd be arriving at my mother-in-law's.'

An old couple were sitting in their modest country cottage talking about their long life together. The shrivelled old woman turned to her spouse and said, 'Tell me, George. There's one thing that's always puzzled me.'

'What's that, dear?'

'Well,' continued the old woman, 'how was it that on such low wages all your life you could afford to buy those two pastures down by the river?'

'It was simple, really,' said George. 'Every time you said "yes" to sex, I put aside a couple of shillings to go towards the land and eventually we could afford it.'

Then he fell silent, deep in thought. After a few moments he added angrily, 'But if I'd done the same when you said "no" instead, we'd have had the whole bloody farm by now!'

'You know, my wife's so ugly,' a miserable husband told his pal over a pint, 'that whenever we have a Peeping Tom round our house, I have to phone him up to apologize.'

First cannibal: **'I hate to say this, but I just don't like my mother-in-law at all.'**
Second cannibal: **'OK, just eat your chips then.'**

Old Mrs Jones, poor thing, once slipped and strained her thigh so badly that her doctor told her not to use the stairs for at least a fortnight.

A couple of weeks later she went to see him again and asked how the leg was healing.

'Very well indeed,' replied the doctor. 'So well, in fact, that you've made a complete recovery and can start using the stairs again.'

'Thank God for that,' replied Mrs Jones. 'That drainpipe's going to be the death of me!'

Old biddy: **'Doctor, doctor — I was told to come here because my eyes need examining.'**
Man in white coat: **'I'll say they do — I'm the bloody butcher.'**

Policeman: 'Is this a recent photograph of the missing person?'
Man: 'Yes, that's my mother-in-law's picture taken just a few days ago.'
Policeman: 'In that case I think we'd better start off by searching all the zoos.'

There's a really rough family living near a mate of mine. A few months back one of them was jailed for beating up the barman in the local. But her grandson reckons she'll be out soon.

Times have been hard down in the country. Recently Farmer Bloggs had to put the pig in with his wife's mother while he looked for somewhere to house it. He thought there'd be hell to pay about the smell, but the pig soon got used to it.

Two women were leaning over the fence chatting one morning and one told her neighbour, 'I bought a new toilet brush at a knock-down price in the discount stall in the market.'
'Is that so?' said the second woman. 'We always prefer to use paper in our family.'

What's the difference between a mirror and typical mother-in-law? One reflects without speaking and the other speaks without reflecting.

An elderly Scots woman was talking to a friend about her English husband. 'He's not really a football fan, ye ken,' she said, 'but he always jumps around a lot if England beat Scotland.'
'Oh yes,' said her friend, 'how long does he keep that up for?'
'Depends how far I kick him,' growled the old Scots woman.

Fred wouldn't have said that his mother-in-law was a big woman, but her legs were so fat, she didn't have calves but cows.

Question: Is it possible to perform major operations on an old woman?
Answer: Yes, but it's much more comfortable on an operating table.

Have you heard what happened to a nagging mother-in-law on holiday with her family in Tenerife. Her tongue got sunburnt.

Which of our Queens was a heavy drinker?
Elizabeth the Thirst.

A couple were walking back to their car after a shopping trip and the wife said to her husband, 'Stop moaning about the weight of those parcels, will you? At least your wallet's much lighter.'

A mate of mine told me that his mother-in-law's finally put herself on a diet. Now she only eats slimmer's bread with her jam and double cream.

One Saturday morning the doorman at the bingo hall noticed that old Mavis was looking a bit downcast as she walked in.

'What's the matter, love?' he asked. 'Anything wrong?'

'Yes, I'm afraid my husband has died,' she replied.

'That's awful,' said the doorman, 'so you had to make your way here by yourself?'

'It's even worse than that,' replied Mavis, 'my son says he can't pick me up today until after the funeral.'

No wonder my mate's mother-in-law looks so bloody scruffy. She says she only changes her clothes when she's down in the dumps.

Dick was a castaway living on a desert island with a beautiful blonde. Over the years they made the best of things and lived together quite happily.

One day Dick came rushing down from the hill with his telescope and told his companion, 'Darling, I've got some good news and some bad news.'

'What's that?' asked the blonde.

'There's a ship sailing into the bay.'

'That's marvellous,' said the blonde. 'What can the bad news possibly be?'

'I've just spotted my wife in the rescue party.'

Did you hear about the unlucky husband who ran over his wife's parents? Poor bloke — his mother-in-law survived.

Fred was chatting to a mate down the pub. 'My wife and I had a terrible row last night,' he said, 'a real humdinger. But at least I had the last word in the matter.'

His friend, who knew Fred's wife was a real old battle-axe, was impressed and asked, 'What did you say to her?'

'All right, buy it,' Fred replied.

Massive Mildred was talking to her down-trodden husband, Bert. 'I feel like buying you a present,' she said to him, 'how much do you want to spend?'

Harry was dumbfounded when his talkative wife finished a telephone call in only ten minutes. 'How did you do it?' he asked.

'Wrong number,' she told him.

A middle-aged woman's husband was impotent and his wife gave him hell. She was always nagging him to 'perform' for her, but it was no good. He just couldn't get it up.

One day it all became too much for him. He stripped himself naked and hanged himself with piece of rope from the chandelier in the hallway.

When his wife came home she found his 'stiff' body hanging there with the familiar hanged man's erection.

'Bloody typical of you!' she stormed at her dead husband. 'The first time you get it up for years and you go and hang yourself.'

After years of feuding Reg decided to make things up with his mother-in-law. So he went to the local pet shop and looked around for a present to buy her. There he saw a very cute-looking white rabbit that was so clever it could tap dance to the tune of 'Singing in the Rain' and perform circus tricks.

'Brilliant,' thought Reg, 'the old lady will be really chuffed with such a gift'.

So he arranged to have the rabbit sent round to his mother-in-law as a surprise present.

The next day Reg phoned his mother-in-law. 'How did you like the rabbit?' he asked.

'Lovely!' said the old woman. 'It was very tasty.'

A middle-aged spinster went to the doctor's one day. 'I wonder if you can help me, doctor,' she said plaintively. 'Can you do anything for these bruises on my knees?'

The GP examined them and said, 'How did you get them?' The woman blushed a bit and then stammered, 'Er, it was from, you know, sex.'

'I see,' said the doctor, 'you did it in the doggie position. Well, the answer's quite simple – you'll just have to change positions for a while until the bruises heal.'

'I couldn't possibly do that,' wailed the woman. 'My alsatian's breath is awful!'

A spinster rushed into a police station. 'Sergeant, sergeant!' she yelled to an officer, 'I've just been graped!'

'Calm down, madam,' said the sergeant gently, 'I think you mean raped.'

'No,' replied the spinster, sobbing. 'There was a bunch of them!'

An old slag walked into a chemist's and asked for five packets of condoms.

'What size would you like?' asked the assistant.

'Oh, various,' she replied. 'I'm not seeing anyone special.'

Two middle-aged sisters run a chemist's shop. One day a young man comes in in a big raincoat looking very embarrassed. He sees one of the women behind the counter, hesitates a few moments before walking out again. The next day the same thing happens. Same man, same coat. He walks in but again sees one of the sisters behind the counter and leaves. The next day the man comes in again and this time plucks up courage and comes over to the counter. 'Excuse me, madam, but you don't have a male assistant I could see, do you?'

'I'm afraid not, young man,' says the sister. 'But my sister and I are both trained chemists, so if you have a problem we can help.'

'Well,' says the man, blushing. 'It's like this.' And he undoes his raincoat to reveal a massive erection, fully ten inches. 'The problem is,' he says, 'I have a permanent erection. What can you do for me?'

'Wait there,' said the woman, 'I'll have to consult my sister.' Two minutes later the woman comes back. 'The best we can offer,' she says, 'is £10,000 a year plus a share of the profits!'

Air hostess to passenger, 'I don't know quite how to break the news, sir – but we've left your wife back at the airport.'

'Thank God for that,' replied the man. 'For a horrible moment I thought I'd gone deaf.'

A butcher was getting increasingly infuriated with a middle-aged woman who was minutely examining a bit of sinewy meat on the counter. She kept prodding and pushing it with her grimy fingers. Finally the butcher lost his patience. 'You're wasting your time,' he snapped, 'it's not like your husband's wotsit – it won't get bigger if you play with it!'

At a meeting of the Women's Institute in the village hall, a well-known explorer was giving a detailed account of a trip to the Amazonian jungle. Eventually the explorer went on to describe the qualities of a particular tribe he had encountered who seemed to have massive 'manhoods'. The explorer even had a few coloured slides to illustrate the point. Well, the atmosphere was beginning to get a bit steamed up in the hall and several of the ladies fidgeted somewhat uncomfortably. Eventually one middle-aged woman could bear it no more, got up and walked out.

The explorer saw the woman as she disappeared through the door.

'There's no need to rush!' he shouted. 'The next plane doesn't leave till Tuesday week!'

A middle-aged woman went to a solicitor's office to ask for a divorce.

'Well, madam, does your husband drink?' he asked.

'No,' she replied.

'Well then, does he gamble?'

'No, he doesn't gamble.'

'Then it must be on the grounds of adultery,' said the lawyer.

'I suppose so,' agreed the woman. 'None of the kids are his.'

Joe was a harassed husband who went into a lingerie shop intending to buy his middle-aged wife a new bra. He didn't really know where to start, but one of the shop assistants was very helpful. There was just one snag – the size!

'Well, what do your wife's breasts look like?' the assistant asked. 'Grapefruit? Melons? Pears?'

Joe replied that they didn't look like any of these.

'Well, what do they look like then?' asked the assistant in desperation.

'Even seen an elephant's trunk?' asked Joe.

Saintly little Louise joined a convent where they had strict rules of silence. Nuns were only allowed to speak two words every five years. After five years it was Louise's turn to utter two words to the Mother Superior. 'Better heating,' she said to the head of the convent.

Five years later and it was Sister Louise's chance again to say those two words. 'Better food,' she told Mother Superior.

Another five years went by and Louise once more came before the Mother Superior. 'Better beds,' she said.

Well, another five years passed and by this time Sister Louise had been at the convent twenty years. She walked into the office for her two words and told the Mother Superior, 'I'm leaving!'

'I'm not surprised,' snapped Mother Superior. 'You've done nothing but moan since you got here!'

Two middle-aged women were swapping notes in a cocktail bar.
First woman: 'I went out with a very wealthy banker last night – and you'll never guess what, he gave me £1,000!'
Second woman: 'You don't say? That's the first time I've ever heard of a £995 tip!'

A young wife was moaning to an old woman one day. 'It's not fair,' said the wife. 'I've been trying with my husband for four years to have a child. I thought all you had to do was sleep with a man once and you got pregnant!'

'Ah yes,' replied the old buzzard sagely, 'but only while you're single.'

An old lady was troubled with a touch of the wind and went to her GP. 'Doctor,' she said, 'I have problems with the wind – I just can't stop producing the stuff.'

The doctor said, 'Well, don't bother about it, lots of people have trouble with the wind.'

'But doctor,' said the old woman, 'mine is totally odourless. It's very odd.'

'Can you do it now?' asked the doctor.

'Oh, yes,' said the old woman. And she dropped a load.

The doctor immediately started writing out an appointment card for a consultant.

'You need an operation as soon as possible,' said the GP.

'On my bowels?' said the old woman.

'No – on your nose,' replied the doctor.

Two pensioners, Joyce and Mavis, were out shopping one day when they popped into a greengrocer's shop. They asked the shopkeeper for two cucumbers.

'Why not buy an extra one,' he said. 'There's a special offer where you get three at a discount.'

The two old women discussed the matter. 'Why not?' said Joyce to Mavis. 'We can always eat the other one.'

Old Jones the farmer had an only daughter, a shrewish middle-aged woman called Nell, who was thought to be frigid. Not surprisingly, she had never married – she had never even kissed a man. One day Old Jones let it be known that if a man could manage to have sex with her, with her consent, he would hand over his estates and money to him there and then.

Well, all the young studs in the neighbourhood tried without success to chat Nell up. She wouldn't have any of it. Then one day a hunky young man called Charles came up and wooed her with flowers, chocolates, the full works. Amazingly it worked and she agreed to sleep with him. But as he got between the sheets he saw her pussy was so small there was no way he would ever get in her. And try as he could he never did, and lost the chance of the inheritance. He was consoled down the pub by his friends later.

'Tell us Charles,' said one. 'How small was it really – like a shell, or a pencil sharpener or what?'

'Ever seen a gnat's backside?' asked Charles quietly.

A woman walks into a pub with a rabbit under her arm. One of the regulars sees her and comments loudly, 'That must be the ugliest bird ever.'

'That's not a bird, that's a rabbit,' retorts the woman.

'I was talking to the rabbit,' replies the man.

A middle-aged Irish woman went rushing to her priest for confession. 'Father, Father, I spent half-an-hour this morning gazing into my mirror admiring my body and thinking how attractive I was. Tell me, do I have to do a penance?'

'No,' said the priest, slightly wearily, 'You only have to perform a penance for a sin. Not a mistake.'

One day a rather mean, menopausal woman swallowed a pound coin by accident. Anxious not to lose the money, she kept a close eye out every time she went to the loo. For three days there was no sign of the money. Then, after four days, she spotted a coin she had passed – but to her astonishment it was only a 50p coin.

'Bloody hell, Bert!' she shouted to her husband. 'I knew I was going through the change – but now the change is going through me!'

A family fell on hard times and one day they decided they would have to sell their few remaining decent things if they were going to survive.

So one morning Old Joe set off to an antiques market with his daughter Minnie. They took the grandfather clock, a diamond brooch and other small bric-a-brac which they were going to sell for the best price they could.

Anyway they were making their way along the highway when misfortune struck and they were attacked by robbers, who took everything the old man and his daughter had.

Old Joe was distraught and wailed it was the end of the family.

'Don't cry, Papa,' said Minnie. 'Look, I've still got the diamond brooch.'

'What?' said Old Joe. 'How on earth did you stop those robbers from getting it?'

'Easy,' said Minnie, 'I hid it up my pussy.'

'Oh, what bad luck!' wailed the old man once more. 'If your mother had come with us we could have saved the grandfather clock as well!'

Two middle-aged women were discussing a mutual aquaintance who had emigrated to America a few weeks before. 'I got a letter from Mary yesterday,' said one. 'She says she got a diamond ring for only fifty bucks.'

'Yes,' snapped her friend, 'Mary never could spell.'

An old woman told a friend she was worried about her eighty-year-old husband's lack of interest in her body. 'Don't worry – that's normal at our age,' said her friend. 'But, look, is there anything in particular that's troubling you?'

'Yes,' said the other woman. 'He hasn't screwed me for four days – I think he's got another woman.'

SACRED
COWS

I did a show once with a whole lot of feminists and every time I mentioned the word 'Ladies' they shouted back 'Women' in protest and refused to let me get away with referring to any of them as 'Ladies'.

To me that sort of attitude is just stupid. I met a real man-hater a while ago who told me that she worked in a garage and wouldn't service a man's car because she loathed men. So I asked her if she felt like that why she dressed like a man with old boots and dungarees, and walking round smoking Old Holborn.

The only answer she had to that was to tell me to piss off. Quite right – rude person.

Women journalists who came to interview me were always trying to find the real Jim Davidson. 'You're not really like that,' they'd tell me and I say, 'I am, I really am. I'm a male chauvinist pig.'

I can't think what a women does better than a man – apart from having babies. That's the thing they always throw back in your face. But it's simple, lying there with your feet up. The worst part is for the fellows who do the watching. The girls don't realize what we blokes have to go through at childbirth. That's why we have to go down the pub and wet the baby's head.

Give an audience of women a line like that, in a jokey way, and you'll soon get a rise out of them.

Have you heard the definition of an intellectual feminist? She's the woman who can dream up excuses that her lover's wife *will* believe.

Did you hear about the upper-class feminist who was into natural childbirth. She didn't wear any make-up.

What's a feminist's nipple? The tip of the iceberg.

What do you call a lesbian prospecting for gold? A Klondike.

Two spinsters were discussing the greatest thrills of their life.
    The first said, 'Mine was when I first saw the sea.'
    The second said, 'Mine was when my Ma gave me an enema.'
    'How come?' asked her companion.
    'She was short-sighted.'

Three long-faced men were swapping notes on how frigid their wives were.
    The first said, 'My wife is so frigid she sleeps with a hot water bottle – and by the morning it's frozen.'
    The second man said, 'Well, my wife's so cold, she goes to bed with an ice cube in her mouth and in the morning she spits it out whole.'
    'That's nothing,' said the third man, 'when my wife opens her legs the central heating comes on!'

What do you get if you cross a cucumber with a pussy? Self-indulgence.

What's the medical term for being a lesbian? Strapa-dictomy.

Joe picked up a hitch-hiker called Sue. After they got chatting it turned out she was a real feminist, but she was also quite attractive and he started thinking how he could have his way with her.

When it was getting dark the car engine started spluttering and fairly soon the car ground to a halt.

'I'm sorry,' Joe said to Sue, 'but it looks as if we have run out of fuel.'

'Don't worry,' replied Sue, and she took a bottle out of her handbag saying, 'I'm sure we can manage.'

Joe's eyes popped out and he thought his luck was in. 'Hey – that's great,' he said, 'what is it beer, whisky?'

'No,' said Sue coolly, getting out of the car. 'It's petrol.'

'I wouldn't say Julie was tough,' Ron told his mate Bill, 'but she used to have to kickstart her vibrator.'

Sophie was well-known as a hard-line feminist but there was no disguising that she was very attractive and had the pick of the men.

Bruce was chatting her up at a party once and thought he was doing fine until Sophie said snootily, 'I ought to tell you that I've now developed immunity to being treated as a mere sex object.'

'That's hardly surprising,' said Bruce, 'after the number of times you've been inoculated.'

Did you hear about the tomboy who wanted to swap her menstrual cycle for a Suzuki?

What's the difference between a pipe-smoking woman and one who's into 'hard sex'? One likes rough shag and the other likes to shag rough.

What have a dildo and soyamix got in common? They're both meat substitutes.

Did you hear about the man who had been married so long even his drinks began to resemble his wife? They were tall, cold and full of gin.

Two girls who had just 'come out' took a room together for their first big night. Both of them were nervous and for a while they giggled a lot and just played around. Then one of them said, 'Look, I want to be earnest for a minute.'

'No, no,' exclaimed the other, 'I want to be Ernest – you can be Bill.'

Why were men invented? Because a dildo can't take a dog for a walk.

A lesbian walked into a sex shop and asked for a dildo.

'Regular, large or extra large?' asked the assistant.

'Extra large,' said the lesbian. 'I want to widen the circle of my friends.'

Did you hear about the lesbian who didn't take sex that seriously? She thought it was just tongue in cheek.

Kid: 'Dad – what's a transvestite?'
Dad: 'Ask Mum – he'll tell you.'

Unable to get home after a busy field trip, a middle-aged woman teacher and an impressionable seventeen-year-old pupil went to find rooms at a hotel. Unfortunately only one bed, a double, was available, so the two of them had to share.

During the night the girl, who had a bit of a crush on her teacher, kept fidgeting and finally said to the older woman, 'Mrs Allen – that dripping tap is keeping me awake.'

Mrs Allen turned dreamily to her companion and answered, 'Look dear, how would you like to pretend to be my husband, just for tonight?'

Her pupil blushed and exclaimed, 'Oh yes, I'd love to!'

'In that case,' snapped Mrs Allen, 'go and turn the bloody thing off yourself!'

Did you hear about the randy woman inventor who combined her vibrator with her Sony radio ... and came up with the first-ever alarm cock?

Tom had the great misfortune to marry a frigid woman to whom sex was merely a duty, and after the children had come there was no more physical contact between them. But Tom was a loyal man and endured his lot, right up to his dying day.

After his death his wife, who went to live in a convent, thought little more of him. But Tom's brother Pete was still upset and decided to go to a medium to get in touch with his brother. After a while the dark silence was broken by the Tom's voice saying, 'Hello, Pete, thanks for getting in touch.'

'Tom, Tom,' cried Pete, 'is that really you? Are you happy?'

'I'm having the time of my life,' replied Tom. 'It's great.'

'Thank goodness,' said Pete. 'I'm so relieved you're having fun in heaven.'

'Who's talking about heaven?' replied Tom. 'I've come back to earth as a ram!'

One morning Mother Superior was walking cheerfully down the corridor when she greeted another nun. 'Good morning, Sister Mary,' said Mother Superior brightly.

'Good morning, Mother Superior,' said the nun quietly. 'You obviously got out the wrong side of bed this morning.'

Mother Superior was puzzled by this remark but thought nothing more of it. Then she passed a second nun. 'Good morning, Sister Anne,' said Mother Superior cheerfully.

'Good morning, Mother Superior,' said the nun a little sheepishly. 'You obviously got out of bed the wrong side this morning.'

Mother Superior thought this was very strange. And when the same thing happened twice more she began to get rather annoyed – she had been feeling rather happy with life up till then.

So when a fifth nun came along and, like the others, remarked, 'You must have got out the wrong side of the bed this morning,' the old nun blew her top.

'Look,' she yelled, 'I was perfectly happy this morning. Why, in the Lord's name does everyone think I got out of bed the wrong side this morning?'

'I think,' said the young red-faced nun, 'it's because you're wearing the matron's apron and stockings . . .'

Did you hear about the sado-masochist lesbian who lost her partner? She was very cut up about it.

Meg was a fifty-year-old woman who was getting married for the first time. She confessed to a close friend that something was bothering her. 'It's sex,' she admitted, 'my only experience was thirty years ago and I don't know how my body will take it.'

Her friend thought about it for a while and then suggested, 'Why don't you practise a few times with a banana?'

So Meg went away and bought a banana to get her ready for marriage. A few weeks later she met her friend again. 'How are you feeling now about the wedding?' she asked.

'Oh, that's all off,' said Meg. 'I bought a crate of bananas instead.'

Two men were discussing what to do about the heat-wave.

'Say, James,' said one, 'did you hear about that new machine they've got which produces ice cubes with a hole in them?'

'Did I hear about them?' said James. 'I bloody married one!'

The girls' school's hockey teacher had just seduced the prim and proper headmistress into her first lesbian activity. Afterwards as they lay together in bed the headmistress started sobbing.

'What's wrong?' said the hockey teacher.

'It's the children on Monday,' sniffed the headmistress. 'After all this wickedness how will I ever be able to face them again?'

'What do you mean, all this wickedness?' said the hockey teacher. 'We've only done it once.'

'I know,' said the headmistress quickly, 'but we've got the rest of the weekend, haven't we?'

Did you hear about the lesbian who lost her sex-drive? Her batteries ran out.

Did you hear about the Eskimo who divorced his feminist wife? Claimed she was too cold in bed.

A man in a pub sticks out his tongue at his friend.

'What the hell do you think you're playing at?' says the friend angrily.

'It's my latest impersonation,' says the man.

'Oh yeah, what of?' replies his friend.

'A lesbian with an erection!'

Hear about the lesbian who moaned about her boss at work? Said he was a right dildo.

BIRD'S EYE VIEW

Having said that women aren't as good as men at various things, in a jokey way, there are a few women like Mrs Thatcher who nearly always get the better of men. I watched her once in Prime Minister's question time, when I went to the Houses of Parliament as a distinguished stranger sitting upstairs in a little gallery. There were people heckling and shouting. Enoch Powell was asleep – I think he did that on purpose just to annoy people, at least that's what someone told me.

The Prime Minister got a really big laugh after Neil Kinnock got up and asked her to answer a long string of questions and when he'd finished she got to her feet and just said 'No'. That brought the house down.

I spoke to her afterwards about it and told her that we had similar jobs. 'Exactly,' she said, 'It's a job and it has to be done.' Prime Minister's question time is more of a tradition than anything else.

American politics is even more of a game. There's Jesse Jackson for one thing. They'll never make him president. They'd have to change the colour of the stamps to start with.

American politics are even more like showbusiness than our own, but we're a bit more dignified. I can't imagine Mrs Thatcher singing 'We'll never walk alone' at the end of her speech with people crying in the audience.

Meeting her was fantastic, a great thrill – you can feel the strength of the lady coming across and it's no wonder most of the men she comes up against aren't a patch on her. She always has the last word and good luck to her and all the other women who get one over on the men. It doesn't happen that often!

A wealthy young businessman picked up a gorgeous girl at a nightclub and took her back to her place for a night of passion.

In the morning, after one of the best nights of his life, he offered to pay her something to show his gratitude.

'There's no need,' she said, 'I don't want any money. But there is one thing you can get for me.'

'What's that?' he asked.

'You can go out and buy me a stainless steel penknife.'

The man thought this was a bit kinky but reckoned he'd got a bargain and so went out to buy the knife. When he returned she told him to put it in a large box in a cupboard.

'Good God,' he exclaimed as he opened the box, 'but this is already stacked with knives – what do you need another one for?'

'It's quite simple,' said the girl. 'I'm young enough now to get any man I want, but when I'm older men won't look at me ... except that Boy Scouts will do anything for a stainless steel penknife.'

A reckless young lady called Alice,
Used gelignite instead of a phallus,
They found her vagina
Aboard a cruise liner,
And the rest of her in Crystal Palace.

Lucy told a friend, 'I'm so tired these days I've had to ration my husband to sex three times a week.'

'That seems quite harsh,' said her friend.

'Not really,' said Lucy. 'I've given up some of my lovers altogether.'

One middle-aged housewife told her neighbour, 'My husband is so thick, he couldn't even manage to be unfaithful to me.'

'How come?' asked her neighbour.

'He went out on the town last week and spent all night in a warehouse.'

A little girl asked her mother, 'Mummy — what's the difference between "Ooh" and Aah"?'
'About three inches,' replied her mother.

Scrawled on the inside of a woman's loo was the message, 'Women of the world stand up for yourselves ... Faint heart never won fur, lady!'

A couple in their nineties appeared before a judge to petition for a divorce. The judge thought it was a bit odd and asked the wife, 'I just don't understand. You're ninety-five, you've been married to your husband now for seventy-five years. Why on earth have you decided to get divorced now?'

'I wanted to wait until all our children had passed on,' said the old woman.

Sophie was telling her friend about the wild party she'd been to the night before.

'It was just so crowded,' she said. 'This bloke was on top of me making love when someone tried to push past in the hallway and stood right on his bum.'

'Really? What did you say?' asked her friend.

'Thank you,' said Sophie.

Carol came home early one day after going out with her handsome new boyfriend.

'What's the matter, why are you home so soon?' asked her flatmate.

'That fellow's got some nerve,' said Carol angrily. 'He just gave me a vibrator and told me to buzz off.'

What's the definition of nymphomania? 'Aye' trouble.

Steve noticed that Jean didn't have any pubic hair and asked her why.

'When was the last time you saw grass growing on a busy street?' she replied.

A bimbo actress called Samantha was being wined and dined by a horny old producer. During the course of the meal she tucked away snails, steak, caviar and lobster, as well as dessert and a couple of bottles of wine. Somewhat stonily the producer said, 'I bet your mother never used to feed you this way.'

Samantha replied, 'No, but then I bet my mother never wanted to screw me either.'

An elderly and saintly priest was making his way to a convent in the city when he found himself approached by a young woman. 'Hey, mister, ten quid for a blow job,' she whispered.

The priest smiled politely and went on his way. Before long the same thing happened again – a woman offered him a blow job for ten quid and he walked on past her.

This happened a few more times before he reached the safety of the convent. After he was inside, he walked up to a young nun who was standing nearby and asked, 'Excuse me, sister, but ... er ... what is a blow job?'

'Ten quid,' replied the nun, 'same as anywhere else.'

Two women were discussing who are more intelligent, men or women.

'Take a man's dick,' said one. 'It's got no brains. It's best friends are both nuts and it lives right next door to an arsehole!'

Mavis and Agnes were looking at a field of animals.

'I wonder why cows always look so sad,' said Mavis.

'Well,' replied Agnes, 'if you had your tits handled twice a day but only got laid once a year, you'd be pretty pissed off too.'

A woman has just discovered a new form of oral contraceptive. She just asks, 'Is it in yet?'

Brian was celebrating his first anniversary with Sophie. 'Darling,' he asked, 'would you still love me if I was injured in a car crash and, you know, I couldn't make love any more?'

'Of course I would still love you,' replied his adoring wife.

'And, darling, if I was horribly disfigured in an accident, would you still love me then?'

Sophie replied, 'Yes, dear. I'd still love you.'

Finally Brian asked, 'Darling, would you still love me if I lost my £100,000 a year job in the City?'

'Of course, darling,' replied Sophie, 'but most of all I'd *miss* you terribly!'

Golda's husband died after thirty years of marriage. Just before the funeral she went to the undertaker and asked if she could have her husband's tool. The undertaker was a bit taken aback but agreed to the request.

A few days later Golda was cooking when her friend dropped by to see her. As they were talking the friend peered casually into the pan and was horrified at what she saw. 'But, Golda,' she exclaimed, 'isn't that Moshe's dick?'

'Yes, it is,' said Golda. 'For thirty years I had to eat it his way – now it's my turn.'

A widow came back from a séance at which she'd made contact with her late unfaithful drunkard of a husband.

'Why are you looking so happy?' a friend asked.

'Because my husband is in heaven with a beautiful blonde and a bottle of Scotch,' replied the widow.

'But what's so good about that?' asked her friend.

'Because the bottle has a hole in it – and she hasn't,' came the reply.

First woman: 'My husband used to be so caring and affectionate – he would really make me feel wanted and desired.'
Second woman: 'So what happened?'
First woman: 'The bloody optician gave him some new glasses.'

John, who suffered from rather small tackle, was on his first date with Sandra. He took her back to his place, turned out the lights, then gingerly directed her hand towards his tiny penis.

'No thanks,' said Sandra, 'I don't smoke.'

Orgasm: **Something men take for granted and prosti-tutes take for advantage.**

An American actress was telling a friend about a trip to Europe where she was wined and dined by the cream of the aristocracy.

'How did it go?' asked a friend.

'Great,' said the actress. 'I managed to make every second count.'

A woman was talking to her friend in the pub and told her, 'I don't like my boyfriend to talk too much – he's got better things to do with his tongue.'

A woman sitting in a cinema went to complain to the manager. 'That man over there. He's been fondling the woman next to him all through the film. And now she's unzipped his flies and has started playing with him. What are you going to do about it?'

'I'm very sorry, madam,' said the manager, 'but they're sitting a long way from you and I don't see why you should be getting so upset. In any case it's not really any of your business.'

'Oh yes it is,' stormed the woman, 'he's my bloody husband.'

On the wall of a women's lavatory someone had written, 'Women must fight for equality with men.'

Underneath someone else had scrawled, 'Why aim so low?'

A girl told her best friend, 'I asked my new boyfriend to kiss me somewhere dirty.'

'What happened?' she was asked.

'He drove me to Barnsley.'

Graffiti in women's lavatory: 'My husband doesn't hold anything against me ... we sleep in separate beds.'

A hard-working wife was hurrying all over her house in a rush to get things clean and tidy for the arrival of her parents-in-law.

Her husband looked up as he lounged reading his paper and said, 'A woman's work is never done, eh love?'

'Not by you it isn't,' sighed his wife.

A man stalled his lurid, customized pink and yellow Volkswagen at a set of traffic lights. As he struggled to restart the engine the lights changed from red to amber to green and back to red again ... several times. Eventually a burly W-pc arrived at the scene to deal with the traffic jam that was fast building up.

'What's the matter, dearie,' she asked the sheepish driver, 'haven't we got the right colours for you?'

Did you hear about the pimp who had a high opinion of himself? Regarded himself as a crack salesman.

Two women sat in a pub discussing the merits of the latest Hollywood 'beefcake' actor they had just been watching in the nearby cinema.

'I don't think he's all that special,' said one. 'I mean, take away his hair, his physique and his nice eyes and what have you got?'

'My old man,' sighed the other woman gloomily.

Little girl: 'Mummy, what's an orgasm?'
Mother: 'Something your father has in three minutes – and I have in the bathroom afterwards.'

Why can't women park cars? Men keep pointing to their tiny organs and tell them they're 'at least ten inches'.

Three women were discussing what foreplay was like with their respective lovers. The Jewish woman said, 'With me it's always the same – a trip to the stores, an hour of begging, then we get down to it.'

The Italian woman told her friends, 'My lover always says before we make love, "What time is your husband home?"'

Then it was the turn of the Australian woman who commented, 'Bruce just says, "Brace yourself, Sheila".'

Wilkinson, the randy Head of Personnel, eyed the prospective and very curvy secretary and told her. 'OK, you've got the job. Now, how would you like to earn a little promotion?'

As the bishop said to the actress ... I'll try and come more often.

A girl who returned from a holiday in Cornwall horrified her mother when she said that she had hitch-hiked all the way.

'But don't you know how dangerous that is?' exclaimed her mother.

'Oh, I have a foolproof way of dealing with that,' said the daughter. 'I just tell every man who gives me a lift that I'm on my way to the AIDS clinic.'

Susie was breaking the bad news to John. 'I'm sorry, darling,' she told him, 'but we've got to end it here. I've tried hard, but I feel I can never love you.'

John was distraught. 'But that's awful,' he wailed, 'and just when I've won all that money on the pools as well.'

'Then again,' added Susie quickly, 'I could always give it one last try.'

One night Joan's husband went missing and for three months there wasn't a sign of him.

Then one day she got a call from the police asking her to identify a body in the mortuary that they thought might be his. When she arrived the attendant lifted up the sheet to reveal the body of an exceptionally well-hung middle-aged man, which, however, wasn't that of Joan's husband. 'That isn't him,' she said, and burst into tears.

'But if that isn't your husband, why are you crying?' asked the mortuary attendant.

'It's nothing,' said Joan, drying her eyes. 'I was just imagining what it would be like to lose a man with all that going for him.'

A secretary was moaning to her friend about her boss. 'You know,' she bewailed, 'I'm convinced that the way to a man's heart is through his dick.'

'How did you work that out?' her friend asked.

'Well, take by boss. When it's hard, he's so soft-hearted he'll promise me the world,' sighed the secretary. 'But when it's soft . . . he's so hard-hearted he couldn't care less.'

One night Julie was admiring her body in front of the mirror and told her husband, David, 'I saw the doctor today and he said I had the breasts of a twenty-year-old and the legs of a young woman.'

'Sure,' sneered David, 'and what did he say about the forty-year-old arsehole?'

'Nothing ... you weren't mentioned at all,' replied Julie.

One Monday morning Gloria arrived at work in the typing pool dressed up to the nines in a new fur coat, diamond rings, a string of pearls – the works.

'Well – how do you think I look?' she asked her friends.

'Guilty as hell,' replied one.

There was an executive who got rid of his secretary because of her lack of experience. All she knew was typing and shorthand.

Well-stacked Susie got a job as a secretary after failing the typing ... but passing the physical with flying colours.

Mr Walters, the boss, had been trying for weeks to get Samantha, his gorgeous new secretary into bed. He lavished gifts on her, took her out for meals, took her to the theatre ... but all to no avail. Then one day he went right over the top and bought her a shiny new sports car. Later that day he was dictating a letter to her when he said, 'Samantha, your knickers are coming down.'

Blushing deeply, she quickly looked under her hemline and then protested, 'Oh no, they're not.'

'Oh yes, they are,' insisted Mr Walters, 'otherwise that new sports car is going straight back to the garage!'

Have you heard about the prostitute who was filling in her tax return? She told the Inland Revenue she was in the 'Wholesale Business'.

A leading executive had just applied for a super sec. He was astonished when Mandy walked in. Not only did Mandy have the figure of Marilyn Monroe, the brains of a genius and gorgeous breasts, she also typed and took shorthand at record speeds. Thoughts of working late into the night with this vision went through the boss's mind ... until he remembered he was happily married with kids. 'I'm very sorry,' he said as abruptly as he could. 'You just won't do.'

Many leaned over towards him, looking at him seductively with her big brown eyes. 'Won't do what?' she cooed.

She was only an auctioneer's daughter — but she certainly gave lots away.

Did you hear about the group of nuns who switched from candles to cucumbers saying they got fed up with the same thing ... wick in, wick out.

Young Cathy was just getting up from her desk and dashing out of the office when her boss spotted her and yelled, 'Where the hell do you think you're going?'

'I'm going to get my hair done,' she explained.

'You can't get your hair done in my time!' exclaimed her boss, furious at the idea.

'Why not? It grew in your time,' said Cathy, casually strolling out.

Louise was a hard-bitten estate agent showing a young couple around a new show house that was still being finished off. She outlined all the advantages: good location, smart exterior and so on. The husband said they liked the place. But he added, 'How strong is it? The whole building seems a bit shaky to me.'

'Don't worry,' replied Louise soothingly. 'It's just that they haven't put up the wallpaper yet!'

Frances was a pretty but empty-headed young secretary. One day she came into her boss's office and asked 'Excuse me sir, but will I get a rise?'

'Yes, Frances,' replied her boss sympathetically, 'when you do a good job.'

'Damn,' replied Frances, 'I *knew* there was a catch!'

Watkins was glaring at his watch as secretary Susie strolled into work. 'You should have been here at eight!' he growled.

'Why?' she asked. 'What happened?'

A man rushed into his lawyer's office.

'I want a divorce from my wife because of her disgusting habits.'

'OK,' asid the solicitor, 'what are the disgusting habits?'

'I'd rather not say,' said the man. 'They're too horrible.'

'You must tell me,' said his solicitor. 'Otherwise the divorce can't go ahead.'

'Well, it's like this,' said the man. 'Every time I go to piss in the sink I find it full of dirty cups and saucers!'

There was a guy who said he could read women like a book . . . he used Braille.

A man went to his doctor and complained that his sex life was dull. 'It's always so boring making love to my wife, there's no variety.'

'Try surprising her,' suggested the doctor. 'Catch her unawares some time and you'll soon find it'll sparkle up your love life.'

So the man went away and planned his surprise. The next morning he bought champagne and a dozen red roses and rushed home. He burst into the house, threw himself on her and began to make passionate love to her.

The next day the man went back to his doctor. 'Well, how did it go?' asked the GP.

The man described what happened but added, 'I did my best but it ended up as boring as ever. In fact, I think the only ones to enjoy it were the other women in my wife's coffee group who sat watching!'

And the Eskimo girl who slept with her boyfriend ... when dawn came she found she was six months pregnant.

Two girls were discussing contraception.

'I find the pill is the best method.' said one.

'Really?' said the other, 'I always use a tin can with a few pebbles inside it myself.'

'What!' exclaimed her friend. 'How the hell does that work?'

'Easy – I just shove it up my boyfriend's backside and when it starts to rattle I tell him to get out!'

Colonel Bufton was on his way home from Kenya after years in the colonial service there. He contacted his wife back in England to say when he'd be back. She was in a panic, because in her husband's absence she'd sought comfort in the arms of Chalkie from down the road – with the result that she now had a young black child. But as she was making arrangements for what to do about this she saw to her horror her husband walking up the path. He'd caught an earlier flight to 'surprise' her.

Quickly she thrust the little black boy into a cupboard as her husband walked into the door.

'Darling, so good to see you!' he said. 'Let me just hang up my coat and we can go upstairs to bed.'

So the Colonel opened the cupboard to hang up his coat, and to his amazement saw the little black boy beaming up at him. 'My God...!' he exclaimed.

His wife, totally distraught, said, 'I'm so sorry!'

'Me too, darling,' replied her husband. 'But how on earth did the little bugger manage to follow me all this way?'

Isn't it nearly opening time ... as the bishop said to the actress.

A woman walked into her GP's dressing-room and started to take her clothes off. 'I don't get it,' she said to another naked woman who was in the room. 'I only came here for a throat infection and I'm asked to strip off.'

'*You're* surprised!' exclaimed her companion. 'I'm only here to sell a new range of drugs!'